SATORI LIVING

How to Create A
Balanced Life That You Love

WHAT PEOPLE ARE SAYING

"I'm a passionate believer in the importance of connecting the physical, mental, emotional and spiritual aspects of life - and since reading *Satori*, I've been amazed by Carol's ability to help readers weave these elements together in everyday life. Her techniques are practical and powerful. Give it a read and you'll be astonished at the results, as you transform from that frustrating 'I should do this,' 'I wish I could do that' mentality to a focused, productive and effective state of being. It's a masterpiece!"

- Kathy Smith, America's Leading Fitness Expert

"Did you ever get the feeling that your life was out of control? I'll bet you never even let the thought slow you down. Neither did I. Not until life knocked me down: an instant awakening. The Japanese call it Satori. I decided it was time to pay a little more attention to myself and the reckless, lopsided life I led. Carol Gutzeit put me on the road to a more harmonious existence. With the Satori Lifestyle Program she can do the same for you. Make the commitment."

- Valerie Voss, Former CNN Senior Meteorologist
and TravelGuide Host

"I have personally experienced Carol Gutzeit's Satori Lifestyle Program, and I feel honored to endorse her book. She combines a deep knowledge of physical fitness training with the wisdom of the heart—creating a unique program that serves a wide range of individuals, from serious athletes to the most fitness challenged. Carol's work provides a powerful tool for those who are ready to live at a new level of optimum health and joy."

- Alice Anne Parker, Author of *Understand Your Dreams*
and *The Last of the Dream People*

"Carol Gutzeit has created a "How To" manual on the creation of a lifestyle that promotes physical health and emotional well-being as byproducts of good old-fashioned "fun." In a day and age where "adultism" has replaced an authentic joy for living, Carol's approach is a breath of fresh air! I recommend her program to everyone who has a body, regardless of gender or age."

- Dr. Sunny Massad, Psychologist

"Carol Gutzeit lives her life joyfully. She is the kindest person I have ever met. Her gentle, nurturing instructions enabled me to shift from being unmotivated to exercise to being enthused and energetic. *Satori* has helped me to develop the discipline I need to create more balance in my life."

- Fauna Hodel, Film Producer

"I cannot speak too highly of the level of excellence and enthusiasm that Carol Gutzeit brings to the area of Mind-Body health and fitness. Since founding Satori Hawaii in 1989, Carol has successfully introduced thousands to their hidden capabilities and talents, unlocking the door to untold potential. The positive impact that her program delivers to participants stands as testimony to her ability to communicate and inspire others. Her book will be a breath of fresh air, bringing these effective concepts of Satori into millions of lives."

- Dr. Patricia Mather, Hawaii Nei Holistic Health Practice

"Do you want the answer? Carol Gutzeit has found it! The Satori Lifestyle Program is an absolutely reliable and revolutionary pathway to ultimate energy, fitness, focus, strength, endurance, confidence, accomplishment, health, peace, happiness and abundant personal insights. Her book will turn a page in your life. It is a dynamic program which will bring you instant exhilaration. It is the answer we have all been looking for."

- Kenneth J. Orton, President OCS International, Inc.

"The 30-day Satori Program changed my life! I have struggled with extra weight as well as aches and pains from a broken ankle and fractured shoulder. Now I wake up knowing I have Satori Yoga to ease the pain. The Satori Yoga video demonstrates yoga poses with modifications for people like me who may never have tried yoga before. I'm more agile, more confident and feel healthier overall. I encourage you to sign up for this program, especially if you're overweight. The nutritional coaching is phenomenal, and it's so convenient to exercise in the comfort of your home. Thank you to the Destination Satori staff for helping me reclaim my health! If somehow you think yoga isn't for you, first experience Satori Yoga. My results amaze me!"

- Amy Amaral - Parksville, NY

"Carol's Satori Lifestyle Program has been life-changing for me! The most surprising aspect for me was that I came away with a profound feeling of love and support in my life. I was looking for empowerment, to take care of myself in all ways, with balance. Balancing female, male energies— balancing the physical, mental, emotional spiritual. I now have a wonderful "practice" to do every day to connect and balance on all these levels, and now know love and support of this in my life. I use these modalities every day and have learned to trust, to be more aware, to manage my thoughts better, and am better able to connect to and balance all aspects of my life.

- Jackie Wilson - San Luis Obispo, CA

satori

L I V I N G

How to Create
A Balanced Life That You Love

by Carol Gutzeit

Photography by Nancy November Sloane

The information in this book is intended as a guide to help readers make their own
discoveries on how to attain and sustain a healthy, balanced lifestyle. As with any
program, you get what you put into it; results may vary.

This book is dedicated to:

My children - Chris, Dawn, and Nichole - who have always been
a source of joy and inspiration;

Everyone who has believed in me and the Satori Living message;

You, the reader.

ACKNOWLEDGMENTS

I would like to express my appreciation to my editor, Nancy Sloane, for her talent and contribution in editing, photography, and graphic design. She turned "Satori Living" into a beautiful work of art by adding her creativity to each page. I would also like to thank Stacey Bickler for her grace and beauty in modeling each illustration throughout the book. She is the first person I certified in Satori Yoga™, and she teaches the practice with great love and devotion.

Special thanks to Melissa Costello for writing the Foreward to this book and for contributing her knowledge on nutrition to the "30 Days to a Balanced Life" online program. The recipes in her books, *The Clean in 14 Detox* and *Karma Chow,* are a delicious addition to the Satori lifestyle.

I'd like to thank fitness icon Kathy Smith for being so supportive over the years and for being such a fan of Satori. She is an inspiration to me, and I appreciate her added wisdom and contribution to the 30-day online program.

I want to acknowledge my family for being such a source of inspiration and support. When my father read the first edition of this book many years ago his response was "Brilliant!" and that meant the world to me. My brother Richard Yaco, a gifted artist, created the Satori logo.

A heartfelt thanks to all who have contributed their resources of time, money, and talent to help me get the message of "Satori Living" out into the world.

I appreciate the use of photos provided by Nancy Sloane, Nichole Gutzeit, and Kathy Smith for the Satori Wisdom messages in the 30-day program.

I thank you, my readers, clients, and friends who have encouraged me to keep writing, coaching, and living life to the fullest.

CONTENTS

FOREWARD by Melissa Costello   10

INTRODUCTION   13
    Satori Principles   17
    Lifestyle Assessment   18

THE SATORI LIFESTYLE   22
    Physical Balance   23
    Mental Wholeness   35
    Emotional Harmony   41
    Spiritual Freedom   48

SATORI YOGA   54
    Energetics   54
    Masterminding   71
    Emotionalizing   72
    Innercises   76

STRESS RELIEF PROCESS   78

THE COMMITMENT   79

30 DAYS TO A BALANCED LIFE   80

ABOUT THE AUTHOR   112

FOREWARD

BY MELISSA COSTELLO
Celebrity Chef, Author, Healthy Living Advocate

As a certified nutritionist, healthy food chef, and advocate of preventative living, most of my clients initially come to me looking to lose weight, wanting a special diet plan or sometimes even the next quick fix. This makes sense, because I am after all a nutritionist. Yet I know from my own journey over the course of these last 25 years, that health is a much larger picture than what you put in your mouth, or how much weight you are losing.

When I begin working with my clients, I need to know about their life as a whole, not just as it's related to nutrition and diet. And, although these two things are extremely important in being healthy, what I usually find is that most people are struggling to feel balance and joy in their lives because they are stressed out, overworked and disconnected from themselves and others.

It seems that the stressors of day-to-day life are the most challenging for many. Or there may be a very important area of their life that is not tended to, like emotions, or spirituality, thinking that those two things have nothing to do with health, balance or being happy. By nature, humans are usually good at focusing on the external aspects of life, like our kids, our jobs, our friends, anything that is outside of us that distracts us from really diving deep into our own life. I used to be one of those people too.

What I learned through my own journey, and years of seeking outside of myself, is that changing my behavior, habits and lifestyle from the inside/out was the only way to peace, serenity and balance. And what I also learned is that this way of living takes focus, intention, acceptance and love; it's a daily practice.

Just as we would brush our teeth every morning, we need to instill what Shawn Achor, author of *Before Happiness* calls, "happiness hygiene." Finding balance in all areas of our lives and staying connected to ourselves needs to be a hygiene; a daily practice, if you will.

This practical and refreshing book provides just that. Carol has beautifully laid out a simple and effective way for the reader to bring their life into balance through the daily integration of the 11 Satori Principles. By assessing where you are currently, using awareness practices to help you shift your focus, and providing simple and practical action steps on how to nurture all four realms of your being - physical balance, mental wholeness, emotional harmony and spiritual freedom - you will experience not only an internal shift in your life, but an external one as well.

Stress management is a key component of this book, and one that is necessary if you are a human walking this earth today. Stress is something that mostly all of us suffer from, and it can lead to disease, illness and depression. Carol's simple breakdown of the three S's - Sources, Symptoms and Solutions - support the reader in actually reducing stress in the moment. By engaging this practice regularly when feeling stressed, the reader will experience a more satisfied, productive, relaxed and balanced way of living.

The beautifully crafted Satori Yoga™, which includes multiple breathing exercises, a specific yoga sequence, self-massage, deep relaxation, masterminding and more, is the foundation of living a Satori Lifestyle. The 30-day program included in the book gives you practical ways to implement the tools and practices of this lifestyle with specific daily rituals and focus. It's almost too easy.

Whatever your journey, I know that Satori Living will not only help you find ease and balance in your life, but will also provide profound shifts that make it impossible to go back to your old way of life.

Melissa Costello
Founder, Karma Chow
Author, *The Karma Chow Ultimate Cookbook*
Wellness Coach, Celebrity Chef
and Culinary Nutritionist
karmachow.com

INTRODUCTION

western culture has been largely focused on the

external world with the belief that materia

abundance holds the key to happiness. As a

result, we have become a society of "doers" with

achievement and financial reward as the barometers

by which we measure our self-worth.

When our idea of success is elusive or fails to bring

us the deep sense of satisfaction we anticipate, we

fall into a state of unease that often shows up as

depression, addiction, anxiety, loneliness, divorce

infertility, poverty, or illness.

Although material things can certainly bring us

pleasure, they alone cannot create the sense of

satisfaction that a well-balanced life provides

Without integrating fully developed mental

emotional, and spiritual dimensions into our physica

world, we may always feel as though something isn't

quite the way we want. A new paradigm is required

one that supports, integrates, and equally values our physical, mental, emotional, and spiritual dimensions.

We begin life in a natural state of balance, wholeness, harmony, and freedom, being and loving with ease, hearts open, feeling safe and secure. As the years pass and we begin to acquire self-awareness, our sense of self, or the "ego," develops as a result of experiencing who we are through the eyes of others. If we are fortunate to be mirrored as smart, attractive, talented, etc., we adopt these beliefs about ourselves. However, our experiences, which universally include loss, failure, and disappointment, also create fear, doubt, and worry about having and being enough. We are reprogrammed out of our blissful state of being into a condition of doing in order to get what we believe will bring us what we need to be happy. Once we recognize and acknowledge that the sum of our beliefs, choices, and actions equals the quality of our lives, we can address the feeling that something is missing, and create the life we imagine and desire.

Satori is a Zen Japanese word that describes the instant awakening that occurs when the body, mind, heart, and spirit are in their natural state of balance and harmony. When these four parts are strengthened and aligned, they work interdependently to create a feeling of elation and harmony. This feeling is similar to what athletes, artists, and musicians describe as "being in the zone" where everything flows with ease, and a chemical endorphin "high" is experienced. With training and mindful practice, Satori teaches us how to achieve and sustain this feeling of exhilaration.

We all have male and female energy. Masculine energy is expressed in the physical and mental aspects of ourselves, while the feminine manifests through the emotional and spiritual parts. Male energy is active and powerful. Female energy is receptive and is the source of our wisdom. We need a balance between both to be in harmony with ourselves and others. When inner wisdom is guiding personal power, the ego takes a back seat and life becomes a joyful experience rather than a struggle.

Satori Living creates positive change through self-awareness and re-conditioning. It helps you create a balance between your male and female energies. It will show you how to investigate your thoughts when uncomfortable feelings arise as they inevitably do. It will train you to observe your egoic mind, reassure and take charge of your ego rather than let it be in the driver's seat. It will give you specific tools to rewire your physical, mental, emotional, and spiritual parts in order to unblock the natural flow of energy available to you to live free of the negative power of stress.

Creating a balanced, fulfilling life is similar to building a home. First you need a plan. Then

you must build a strong, stable foundation - your physical self. From there you can create a structure that sets boundaries and provides the framework through which you view the outside world - your mental self. Next you create the interior space by furnishing and decorating in a way that makes you feel good and expresses who you are - your emotional self. Ultimately you move into your home and it becomes a sanctuary for your well-being - your spiritual self. As you can see, if you leave any of these four parts out, your home will be incomplete. Likewise, if you don't pay attention to any one of these four aspects of yourself, you will feel like something is missing.

THE SATORI LIFESTYLE IS BORN

It was during my quest for physical fitness that I had my first Satori moment and launched Satori Hawaii, Inc. Being physically fit gave me a sense of personal power. I was passionate about fitness and chose to become a certified fitness professional early on in my career. I focused on physical fitness for 10 years until one day while playing tennis, I stepped back on a ball and was knocked off my feet, twisted and severely sprained my ankle. While recovering, it became clear to me that there was an imbalance in my life. With all the attention I was giving to my physical body, there wasn't much time for mental, emotional, or spiritual growth. I realized I needed a way to train all four parts in order to be totally fit.

Out of that epiphany, the Satori Lifestyle Program was born. ("Satori" represents the Eastern tradition of living in harmony. "Lifestyle" defines the way we choose to live our lives.)

The Satori Lifestyle Program has been the foundation of my life since starting Satori Hawaii, Inc. in 1989. The program offers a daily practice and practical, step-by-step guide to balancing your physical, mental, emotional, and spiritual parts in order to manifest a joyful, fulfilling, and healthy life. It's a process that will lead you away from fear and back to love, your natural state.

This book is for anyone who is ready to embark on a journey of self-discovery and dares to awaken. I invite you to take the first step by simply being open to the possibility that when you change the way you look at life, life responds with positive change. As you begin this journey, remember to be patient with yourself. It took many years to be programmed and conditioned out of your natural state of being. Without a healthy discipline, the mind and body can become a prison of negative thoughts. Simply by setting the intention to awaken to a balanced life, you will begin to create one that is more joyful and fulfilling.

I hope the Satori Lifestyle Program inspires you to take charge of your life. You have the power to create whatever you choose!

Satori Principles

1.   Life is energy.

2.   We thrive on a balance of physical, mental, emotional, and spiritual energy.

3.   Balance leads to harmony and creates the foundation for an optimal quality of life.

4.   We shape our bodies and our lives with energy.

5.   A state of balance and harmony can be developed through training.

6.   Physical energy is increased by releasing internal blocks of tension.

7.   Mental energy is enhanced by the positive use of our imagination and focused attention.

8.   Emotional energy is stimulated through understanding and healthy expression.

9.   Spiritual energy flows freely through acceptance, trust, gratitude, and love.

10.   LOVE (Living On Vital Energy) is the source of freedom.

11.   The decision to be in harmony with yourself and your physical world can happen instantly . . .

satori !

Lifestyle Assessment

The first step on this journey is to look at your life on four levels and assess where you are right now. The following Lifestyle Assessment will help you evaluate what needs the most attention, determine what is working for you, and identify what needs to change. You may want to invite a friend to go through this process with you.

If you feel that the statement is true for you and your life in general, circle the point value next to it. Add them up to get your lifestyle profile.

PHYSICAL

    1 pt.   I am comfortable with my body. I like the way it is.

    1 pt.   I am in good health.

    2 pts.   I am fit. I have strength, flexibility, and endurance.

    1 pt.   I exercise at least 20-30 minutes three times per week.

    1 pt.   I feel good about what I eat.

    1 pt.   I enjoy eating.

    1 pt.   I am within 10% of my ideal weight. (Use the following as a guide)

Ideal weight for women: 100 pounds for the first five feet of height and five pounds for every inch over five feet. For example: a woman 5'4" tall would have an ideal weight of 100 + 5 x 4 = 120 pounds. Add 10% for a heavy frame and subtract 10% for a small frame. Ideal weight for men: 106 pounds for the first five feet of height and six pounds for every inch over five feet.

    1 pt.   I drink two cups or less of caffeinated beverages per day.

    1 pt.   I don't drink alcohol or I drink moderately.

    1 pt.   I don't use recreational drugs or tranquilizers.

    1 pt.   I enjoy nighttime sleep, usually six-to-eight hours without resorting to tranquilizers, sleeping pills, or alcohol.

    1 pt.   My sleep is restful and I wake up feeling refreshed.

    1 pt.   I do not feel threatened or get tense about my physical well-being.

    1 pt.   I have plenty of energy.

    TOTAL: _____

MENTAL

1 pt.   I usually see the bright side of things.

1 pt.   I usually perceive problems as potential opportunities.

1 pt.   I do not feel threatened or get tense about my psychological well-being.

1 pt.   I do not feel threatened or get tense about my financial well-being.

1 pt.   I do not feel threatened or get tense about minor hassles of life, such as getting caught in traffic, someone being rude to me, missing an appointment, deadlines, etc.

1 pt.   I am flexible, and can adjust to change easily.

1 pt.   I am not rigidly attached to my idea about how things have to be.

1 pt.   I enjoy challenges.

1 pt.   I am able to commit myself to a specific task, project, or job.

1 pt.   I am mentally active. I enjoy reading, writing, problem solving, and keeping up with what is happening in the world.

5 pts.   I love my job.

TOTAL: _____

EMOTIONAL

1 pt.   I am generally happy.

1 pt.   I don't have any debilitating fears.

1 pt.   Fear of aging does not dominate my mind.

1 pt.   I have a happy family life.

1 pt.   I enjoy friendships.

1 pt.   I get along with my peers in the workplace.

1 pt.   I do not feel threatened or get tense about my emotional well-being.

1 pt.   I express how I feel in a healthy way.

1 pt.   I find occasion to laugh every day.

1 pt.   I am able to laugh at myself.

5 pts.   I have moments of pure joy (bliss) without a reason.

TOTAL: _____

SPIRITUAL

1 pt.   My self-talk (the conversation that goes on in my head) is dominated by the theme "What can I do for others?" rather than "How can others help me?"

1 pt.   I like to get involved in community or global activities.

1 pt.   My home is a peaceful sanctuary.

2 pts.   I have a spiritual practice.

2 pts.   I know my life purpose.

1 pt.   I spend time in nature at least once a week.

2 pts.   I trust my intuition.

5 pts.   I am able to enjoy inner silence on a regular basis.

TOTAL: _____

SCORING

Add up your points in each category:

Physical	_____
Mental	_____
Emotional	_____
Spiritual	_____

Add all points together: TOTAL SCORE   _____

46 points and above:	Exceptional
40 - 45 points:	Excellent
30 - 40 points:	Good. You need to pay attention to the missing factors in order to enjoy an optimal quality of life.
Below 30 points:	You may want to seriously consider rethinking and restructuring your priorities in life.

What is your life purpose? _____

_____

_____

How would you describe yourself on these four levels? Use the lifestyle assessment to help you get clear.

PHYSICALLY I AM _____

_____

_____

MENTALLY I AM _____

_____

_____

EMOTIONALLY I AM _____

_____

_____

SPIRITUALLY I AM _____

_____

_____

If you were to live your life more fully, what is the first change you would make?

_____

_____

_____

_____

THE SATORI
lifestyle

"I have learned never to underestimate the capacity of the human mind and body to regenerate — even when prospects seem most wretched. The life force may be the least understood force on earth."

— Norman Cousins

It's Up To You

Have you ever wondered why you make the choices you do? Are your decisions based on what you want or what someone else wants? Do you even know what you want? If you know what you want, why don't you have it? When you get what you want, are you happy? If you are not happy when you get what you want, then what is happiness?

You always have a choice about how you live your life. When you choose to be happy about being alive, no matter what challenges come your way, you can address life from a centered state of inner strength, joy, peace, and harmony. Obviously this is easier said than done. It is helpful, however, to remember that you are a human being, not a human doing. You always have control over your inner state by the way you use your energy. Energy that is flowing feels good. Energy that is blocked feels bad.

Just as you wake up every morning and start a new day, you can wake up every day and start a new life, one that fits your unique style, and expresses all your talents and gifts. It's time to wake up and live your life to the fullest by accepting yourself in this moment. Acceptance invites change to happen naturally as you learn and grow from your life experience. You are unlimited. Life is an opportunity to know that truth.

The four states of well-being that support your health, happiness, and peace of mind are: physical balance, mental wholeness, emotional harmony, and spiritual freedom. You are about to learn how to remove the blocks of stress, worry, fear, and doubt that inhibit the flow of energy to your body, mind, heart, and spirit. When your physical, mental, emotional, and spiritual parts are energized and properly aligned, greater joy, peace, and fulfillment will be yours!

Physical Balance

Everything in the universe is composed of energy. Human beings are energy forms that thrive on balance. Using stimulants like caffeine, sugar, nicotine, and certain drugs will artificially boost energy while depressants like alcohol and tranquilizers provide the opposite effect to calm the energy down. Chronic stress, which is caused by our resistance to what has happened or our fear of what might happen, throws us off balance and depletes our energy. Stress stems from the belief that we can control what happens to us when in fact, the only thing we can control is our response to what happens and our thoughts about the past or future. The more we resist what is and fear what might be, the more we respond from an egoic center, which is our distorted perception of reality. When we operate from this fear-based perspective, it triggers emotions that cause us to behave in any number of negative ways. Thus begins the endless cycle of life spiraling downward in the physical realm.

The way in which we choose to live affects not only the quality of our life today, but also what we attract into our lives over time and how we age. Our lifestyle choices not only contribute to our physical well-being, but also affect our mental and emotional health which is reflected in the way we look and feel. Evidence points to hundreds of studies that demonstrate a connection between emotional well-being and physical health. It is a well-known fact that chronic stress causes illness.

Chronic stress creates a build-up of tension in the body that constricts the flow of life force energy. Stress is a form of resistance. To prevent this from happening it is useful to accept life as it is. That doesn't mean that things can't change from that moment on. It means that if it has already happened there's no point in resisting. You can waste a lot of energy resisting what is. When you're stuck in your head, occupied with past and future thinking, you are literally missing all the present moments that make up your real life.

Take a moment right now to bring your hands in front of your chest and press them together with all your strength. After several seconds, notice how you feel. If you did this throughout the day, it would wear you out! This is no different than what occurs when you resist what is happening in your life. You may start to feel some tension in your neck and shoulders, a headache, backache or upset stomach. If these symptoms are not addressed, then the tension constricts your life force energy and on and on it goes until more serious symptoms show up to get your attention. Your body is the physical manifestation of your thoughts and emotions. If you want to change the way your body feels, start by changing the way you think moment to moment. The way you choose to respond to whatever is happening in your life will either make you feel good or bad.

Are you resisting the present moment? Are you so preoccupied with the past and future that you miss the present? Living in the present moment is one of the most challenging things for the Western mind to do, and it is one of the most important things we need to learn in order to experience joy. Life is happening in the present. When you resist the present you create stress. You can reduce or eliminate this source of stress simply by choosing to live fully in the moment.

You may be wondering how this is possible. Your mind has the ability to jump around into the past and future as if they were real while your body always remains in the present. By consciously connecting your mind with your body, you can keep your mind in the present moment. The simplest way to do this is to breathe consciously. Since breathing is both an automatic and controlled function of the body, you can connect with your body by controlling the depth of your breathing and being aware of your breath as you go about your day.

Another useful way to be present is to come to your senses. Use your body's five senses to really see what you are seeing, taste what you are eating, hear the sounds in your environment, smell the fragrances of nature, and touch more things and people during the day (hugs are great stress reducers).

There are three sources of stress: 1) your environment; 2) your body; and 3) your thoughts.

ENVIRONMENT

Your environment is anything outside of you that you cannot control. Things like traffic, weather, and other people create all sorts of conditions we may not like but can't control. What you can control is your response. When you are fully grounded and balanced within yourself, you can remain calm no matter what is happening in the outside world. This is the source of your power. The moment you allow what is happening to take you out of your center, you have given your power away to someone else.

THE BODY

Your body can become a source of stress when you don't give it the attention it requires. All physical symptoms are messages. For example, just as you would feed your body when you are hungry, if you're feeling tired, carve out time for rest. If you're feeling tension in your body, get a massage or go to a yoga class. Pay attention to your physical body. It knows what it needs and is trying to tell you. If you ignore these signals repeatedly over time, larger issues may begin to appear.

THOUGHTS

Your thoughts can also be stressful when you focus on what is going wrong in your life. Simply by shifting your attention to what is going right in the moment helps to reduce stress instantly.

Stress does have a purpose, however. It triggers a fight-or-flight response with a whole series of chemical reactions in our bodies to help us survive a life-threatening situation. This was useful for our primitive ancestors who frequently faced real physical danger. In the modern world, the dangers we face might feel life-threatening, but they usually don't require us to fight or run away in order to survive.

According to *The Joy of Stress* by Peter G. Hanson, M.D, stress causes:

- A release of cortisone from the adrenal glands to prevent an allergic reaction
- An increase of thyroid hormones that speed up the metabolism to provide extra energy
- A release of endorphins, the "feel good" hormones, that act as a pain killer

- A reduction in sex hormones - testosterone in the male and progesterone in the female - to prevent distraction
- The shutdown of the digestive tract to divert blood to the muscles
- Sugar to be released along with an increase in insulin for a quick energy supply
- Cholesterol in the blood to be increased to supply long distance fuel for muscles
- The heart to beat faster to pump more blood to the muscles and lungs
- Breathing to become deeper and more rapid to supply oxygen to the blood
- The blood to thicken to increase the capacity to carry oxygen, fight infections, and stop bleeding from a wound
- The skin to "crawl," pale, and sweat to detect danger, reduce blood loss, and cool overheated muscles
- The senses to become more acute to bring the body into peak performance

When these responses are not used the way nature intended, as in "fight or flight," they can rob you of vital energy rather than increase it.

The Stress Response

I remember experiencing the fight-or-flight response right before the start of my first triathlon in Hawaii. We were lined up on the shore in Waikiki waiting to start the swim portion of the competition. I'd heard horror stories about how serious triathletes would swim right over the novices. Just the thought of jumping into the ocean and swimming out around a buoy with all these serious-looking athletes caused my heart to beat so hard that I could see it pounding in my chest. The gun went off signaling the start of the race and I could feel the surge of adrenaline shooting through my body. I felt the fear and still managed to dive into the Pacific Ocean and begin the race. I survived the swim with a couple of kicks to the head, but no one actually swam over me. There was a strong current out by the buoy that seemed to keep me in one place for a long time. But I survived! When I reached the shore I was thrilled to have completed the first round. I quickly got into my biking gear and off I went for the 25-mile bike portion of the race which went remarkably well. Even though I was using a mountain bike I seemed to be passing many of my fellow triathletes. When I got off the bike and started the last leg of the race, a six-mile run, my legs felt like jello. About halfway through the run I noticed that I was moving at a much faster pace than usual, even though my legs were fatigued. I realized later that I had run on all the adrenaline that my body had released from the fight-or-flight response. It was clear to me that short-term stress actually contributed to a higher level of performance. If I had chosen not to race after the stress response, I would have felt fatigued, but instead I felt fantastic!

How to Reduce Stress in the Moment? Look for the Three "S's"

The first step to reducing stress is to recognize the SOURCES. What is causing you to react in a negative way? Next become aware of what is happening with your body, mind, and emotions. There are a variety of common SYMPTOMS such as headaches, muscle tension, fatigue, stomach aches, insomnia, rashes, irritability, anger, depression, impatience . . . the list goes on and on. The third step is to have SOLUTIONS. Prevention is always the best way to take care of your health. Ideally, you need to be so in tune with your body that you release tension before it causes more symptoms. When you are aware of chronic symptoms, you can identify the source in order to deal with stress in a healthier way.

AWARENESS EXERCISE

1. SOURCES: What are the biggest sources of stress in your life? _____

_____

_____

_____

_____

_____

_____

_____

_____

2. SYMPTOMS: What are your physical and emotional symptoms? _____

_____

_____

_____

_____

_____

_____

_____

_____

_____

3. SOLUTIONS: What do you do to alleviate your symptoms? _____

_____

_____

_____

_____

_____

_____

_____

To return to balance and restore the flow of life force energy, you need to let go of tension. Think of a rubber band that you stretch to the point of tension. If you keep stretching it, eventually it will break. If you release the tension, it will be propelled by the energy of released tension. You are either creating a state of ease or dis-ease by the way you handle stress.

ACTION STEPS

SOURCES: Write a new response for each of your sources of stress that eliminates the resistance.

_____

_____

_____

_____

SYMPTOMS: Identify your symptoms and write down how you can prevent each of them.

_____

_____

_____

_____

_____

_____

SOLUTIONS: When you recognize that you are stressed, what are three new ways you can release the tension?

_____

_____

_____

_____

_____

As you look at the sources of stress in your life, you may discover that you need to make your health more of a priority and make new choices.

You may decide to look at things from a different perspective to accept what is happening and learn from it. With the tools in this book you will be practicing exercises and techniques to reduce stress, release tension, increase energy, and restore physical balance. Refer to Energetics in the second half of this book for step-by-step instructions on breathing exercises, yoga, self-massage, and deep relaxation.

BREATHING

Breathing is a vital source of energy. We can live for several weeks without eating any food, several days without drinking fluids, but we can only survive a matter of minutes without breathing air.

The human body is designed to release 70% of its toxins through breathing. The other 30% are discharged through sweat, urination, and defecation. If you're not breathing efficiently to rid yourself of toxins, other systems of the body, such as your kidneys, must do the extra work. The skin is the body's largest organ and needs life-giving oxygen to look vibrant and healthy. If we are not using the full capacity of our lungs to breathe in oxygen and breathe out carbon dioxide, the skin must help with the elimination of toxins.

You might think that aerobic exercise would supply enough fresh oxygen to your system to keep it healthy. Although

"Improper breathing is a common cause of ill health."
\- Andrew Weil, M.D.

vigorous exercise is extremely beneficial, during aerobic activity, the body actually burns up the oxygen as soon as it comes in. By practicing deep breathing exercises, you are nourishing your body and receiving therapeutic benefits that aerobic activities don't provide. After teaching breathing exercises to a woman with emphysema, she suggested I write a book because the exercises gave her more relief than anything she had ever tried before.

Stress causes shallow breathing. The fastest way to de-stress is to breathe deeply. It is physiologically impossible to breathe deeply and feel stressed at the same time. Therefore, you can immediately change the way you feel by changing the way that you breathe. Breathing consciously is an integral part of every aspect of Satori Yoga™. It is a way of connecting the mind with the body. Inspire means "to breathe in." The deeper we breathe the deeper we live from inspiration.

AWARENESS EXERCISE

Sit in a comfortable position with both feet on the floor, spine straight and shoulders relaxed. Close your eyes and become aware of your breath. Notice where your breathing originates. Place one hand on that part of your body where you can feel the rise and fall of your breath.

ACTION STEPS

The natural, healthy way to breathe is from the abdomen. That means you will feel the rise and fall of your belly as you breathe deeply. Take a deep breath through your nose to the count of four and fill up your lungs, hold it for four seconds, and then let it out slowly through your mouth saying "haaa" to the count of eight. Practice this three more times. Make a habit of taking four deep breaths throughout the day, especially when you feel tense to calm your nervous system. Determine a trigger that will remind you to do this simple stress reduction technique.

YOGA

Dogs and cats instinctively stretch their spines upon awakening. Perhaps if we followed their example, we too would have the energy and flexibility they have to run and play. Since the spine protects the central nervous system, which governs all the organs of the body and the skeletal structure, keeping it flexible for maximum circulation ought to be a top priority. Hatha yoga is a 5,000-year-old tradition for keeping the spine strong and flexible. It was created by ancient yogis who observed animals and nature. Yoga has the power to bring us back to our natural state of being — relaxed and at ease with life force energy (prana, chi, qi) flowing freely.

Yoga means yoke or union. It brings the body and mind together in present moment awareness through the connecting link of the breath. During the practice of letting go of physical

"You are as young as your spine is flexible."

- Ancient Adage

tension through stretching postures, we need to be willing to observe and let go of mental patterns that cause tension. This increase in awareness will help us to still the mind chatter that creates an unnatural state of dis-ease in the body. This is a crucial step towards releasing past patterns of rigid, learned behavior that limit your full natural expression.

Simply by incorporating yoga or stretching exercises into your daily routine, you will notice a tremendous difference in the way you feel. Letting go of tension is particularly effective after deep breathing exercises because the body is warmed up and oxygenated. Deep breathing also clears away brain fog which makes it easier for the mind to stay focused in the present.

I've been practicing hatha yoga for more than 40 years. In the first year I added a half-inch to my height. I know a woman in Hawaii who started practicing yoga at age sixty and grew one-and-a-half inches. She became a yoga instructor in her seventies!

AWARENESS EXERCISE

Body Scan - You can do this either sitting or lying down. Simply close your eyes and bring your awareness to your feet. Notice if there is tension there. Move up into your ankles, calves, knees, and thighs. Bring your attention to your belly and then your lower back. Keep moving your awareness up into your chest and mid-back, then your neck and shoulders, arms and hands. Observe your face for tension, especially the forehead and jaw, and then your scalp.

ACTION STEPS

How will you incorporate yoga or stretching into your daily routine to reduce or prevent tension? Examples:

- I commit to stretching for 15 - 20 minutes after my workout.
- I commit to practicing Satori Yoga™ at least three times this week.
- I intend to buy a yoga DVD.
- I am attending a yoga class this week.

SELF-MASSAGE

Universal energy, known as "chi" in oriental medicine, circulates through channels in the body called meridians. These minute pathways are located beneath the surface of the skin and

"The means whereby man is created, the means whereby diseases occur, the means whereby man is cured, the means whereby disease arises: the twelve meridians are the basis for all theory and treatment." - Nei Ching

contain a free-flowing colorless fluid. There are specific acupuncture points along the meridians which can be massaged, as in acupressure, to stimulate the energy flow in the body. The self-massage in this book combines three techniques:

1. Touch for Health, a process of unblocking energy and restoring balance to the system using acupressure points. This type of massage has the added benefit of strengthening muscles and organs by opening up the energy flow that nourishes them.

2. Therapeutic Massage to release muscle tension.

3. Reflexology uses applied pressure to the hands or feet to promote a relaxation response and increase energy throughout the entire body.

It is extremely beneficial to receive bodywork from a skilled professional on a regular basis—weekly would be ideal. There are a variety of modalities such as Swedish massage, Thai massage, shiatsu, watsu, myofascial release, rolfing, acupressure, acupuncture, chiropractic, etc., that enhance circulation, release toxins, promote relaxation, and instill a sense of well-being. In addition, giving yourself a massage on a daily basis will help maintain and improve health. Self-massage

is a great way to stay connected to your body.

AWARENESS EXERCISE

How often do you take care of your body with a massage or some form of bodywork?

Frequently ____   Sometimes ____

Rarely ____   Never ____

ACTION STEPS

- Choose a form of bodywork that you feel drawn to and make an appointment for a treatment. Make a commitment to do this for yourself at least once a month.

- Practice the self-massage part of Satori Yoga at least three times this week.

- Practice reflexology (massaging hands or feet) on a daily basis.

DEEP RELAXATION

Why is it sometimes difficult to relax and be at ease with ourselves? Do you ever tell yourself

that you "should" be doing something but resist doing it? "I should do this or I should do that to get what I need." This is the work of an over-zealous ego that is always "shoulding" as a way to feel better about itself. The problem with this way of thinking is that the ego is never satisfied for very long. Even when you do everything you think you should do, there is always more to do.

So how do we get the ego to quiet down and stop telling us what we should do so we can relax and enjoy life? Start by letting the tension in your body go. Once this energy is released, it becomes easier to calm your mind.

Deep relaxation offers many benefits. Besides experiencing greater peace of mind, you will also experience the alpha state, one of the electrical brainwave patterns. This produces an altered state of consciousness similar to daydreaming, with the benefits of sleep with a special kind of awareness. It is the state you are in right before you fall asleep and right after you wake up when you are most connected with your right brain, the creative, intuitive side.

You may be thinking that you don't have time during the course of your busy day to devote to deep relaxation. The truth is, it is one of the best uses of your time. 15 to 20 minutes of deep relaxation is equivalent to a three-hour nap. It refreshes and invigorates your body and helps you tap into the creativity of your right brain. Your powers of visualization are 20 times more effective when you are deeply relaxed so it is the perfect time to use your imagination in a productive way. Make sure you won't be interrupted. You may want to listen to soothing music to help you relax.

AWARENESS EXERCISE
On a scale of 1 - 10, where are you now?

1	2	3	4	5	6	7	8	9	10
Relaxed									Tense

ACTION STEPS
Allow yourself at least 10 to 20 minutes a day for deep relaxation, either in silence or with soothing music.

Practice the Deep Relaxation part of Satori Yoga™ at least three times this week.

When you emerge from your state of relaxation, use this creative state of mind to explore new ideas, solve problems, or be spontaneous. This is an excellent time to write your insights in a journal.

"Relaxation is who you really are. Tension is who you think you should be."
- Ancient Chinese Proverb

"Everything is energy and that's all there is to it. Match the frequency of the reality you want and you cannot help but get that reality. It can be no other way. This is not philosophy. This is physics." - Albert Einstein

Mental Wholeness

Your mind can either be your best friend or your worst enemy. It depends on how well you master the power of your thoughts. Thoughts are constantly streaming in and out of your consciousness at a rate of about 60,000 per day.

Your thoughts are like currency. If you were given $60,000 every day to spend on whatever you wanted, would you waste it on junk you don't want? Probably not. You need to be just as conscious with how you spend the energy of your thoughts because your thoughts create your reality.

"Imagination is more important than knowledge."
- Albert Einstein

The mind's greatest tool is the imagination. The only misuse of imagination is worry. If your thoughts are on what you don't want, they are blocking what you do want. Creative energy needs to flow in the direction of what you desire in order to use your thoughts in a positive way.

The mind responds to mental exercise the way the body responds to physical exercise — it becomes stronger, more flexible, develops endurance, and directs creative energy to shape your life with intention.

Getting clear about what you want is the first step towards consciously creating your life. If you were dining at a restaurant and couldn't decide what to order, the server wouldn't bring any food. Similarly, if you don't know what you want in your life, the universe cannot bring it to you.

Step back for a moment and observe your life. Think of it as if you were watching a movie, one in which you are the writer, director, producer, and star. Your mind creates the screenplay, your emotions are the producer, your spirit is the director, and your body performs in all the scenes that make up your life. The challenge is to align your thoughts, feelings, and actions with the higher purpose of your spirit — the director.

AWARENESS EXERCISE

Think of something you want. Close your eyes for a full minute, think about what you want, and observe your thoughts. Do this exercise now before you continue reading.

Did you have only positive thoughts about what you want? It's been determined that about 75% of what we think about is negative. Obviously, thoughts just come so it's important to be aware of them so you can change your focus if you need to. If your thoughts are mostly negative, you will feel bad. If you're experiencing negative emotions, pay attention to what you're thinking. If you feel sad, for example, ask yourself "What is the thought behind this feeling?" You have the power to deconstruct your thoughts and change your feelings from negative to positive.

ACTION STEPS

Whenever you need to change the focus of your thinking from negative to positive, you can ask yourself questions that will evoke a positive response. Write your answers to these four questions right now.

What am I proud of?

What am I grateful for?

What am I looking forward to?

What am I committed to?

Ask these questions any time during the day or before you fall asleep at night. They are also good questions to ask other people to help them focus on what is positive in their lives.

What we focus on expands. If you focus on what you don't like about yourself, other people or your life, you will see more of that. Why not focus on what you do like so you can see more of that? Remember, where your attention goes, energy flows.

When you learn to master your mind you are operating from wholeness because you are using both sides of your brain. The right brain (creative, intuitive, receptive) is the female side. The left brain (logical, analytical, active) is the male side. Both sides working together creates a whole person that knows how to direct power with action and be guided by intuitive wisdom.

REFLECTION

Your life is a mirror of your thoughts. Before your dreams and desires can become a reality, it's useful to have a clear picture of what they are. With these reflection exercises, you will get clear about what you intend to create. Without reflection, the tendency is to keep creating different variations of the same theme. Nothing ever really changes in your life until you change your mind.

AWARENESS EXERCISE

Everything is created twice, first in the mind and then in the physical world.

To declare what you want in writing, and then say it out loud to yourself and another person, is a courageous first step. Whatever comes after the words "I am" is a powerful declaration. We have so many thoughts each day and often they conflict with one another. This process helps you sort through your thoughts to determine which ones you intend to keep and which are no longer useful for manifesting your desires.

Reflection is an important part of mastering your mind because it helps you get clear. Without clarity we keep having the same thoughts that produce the same reality. I recommend the movie *"Groundhog Day"* with Bill Murray to fully understand this concept.

AWARENESS EXERCISE

Close your eyes, take three deep breaths and look at your life on all four levels:

BODY: Your physical health, fitness, energy level, and body image.

MIND: Your job, career, hobbies, activities, and creative projects.

HEART: Your relationships, including self-love.

SPIRIT: Your home, community, contribution to the world, life purpose.

ACTION STEPS

1) Get clear about what you choose to create in each area of your life and write it down.

PHYSICAL (health, fitness, energy, image, material things)

MENTAL (job/career, creative projects, hobbies, activities)

EMOTIONAL (relationships - spouse, partner, children, friends, co-workers, self)

SPIRITUAL (home, community, life purpose)

2) Make a declaration for each area. Anything that comes after the words "I am" is a powerful statement. You can phrase it one of three ways: "I am . . . or "I am willing to be . . ." or "I am creating . . . Choose the one that feels right when you say it so there are no mental blocks.

Examples

"I am healthy and fit."

"I am willing to be healthy and fit."

"I am creating health and fitness."

BRAINSTORMING

This right brain activity stimulates creativity. When you allow yourself to freely associate words that relate to your specific goal, you are getting to your subconscious mind and opening yourself up to what you deeply want.

Choose one goal to begin this process. For example, let's say your first goal is to be healthy and fit. Brainstorming looks like this:

ACUPUNCTURE

SUNSHINE   RAW FOOD

MASSAGE   SAUNA

YOGA   HIKING   SLEEP 8 HRS

SCHEDULE WORKOUTS   SWIMMING

DANCE   DVDs

HEALTHY & FIT

DETOX   PILATES

GREEN SMOOTHIES   MOUNTAIN BIKING

BREATHING   WEIGHT LIFTING

FUN   BALANCE   EAT MORE GREENS

WORKOUT BUDDY   TENNIS

Brainstorming Exercise

Write what you want in the center of a sheet of paper and surround it with the words that come to mind and circle them. This may include people, places, things to do, feelings, etc. Do this exercise freely without analyzing your thoughts.

Written Description

Now use the words from your brainstorming session to write a description of what this looks like in your life. Start with your declaration, be clear and use your left brain (logical side) to organize your thoughts into a mental picture of what you desire with as many details as possible.

VISUALIZATION

Visualization is creating a mental picture of what it is you want. When you spend time visualizing, you are sending out magnetic energy that attracts what you imagine. It's 20 times more effective to visualize when you are relaxed than when you are tense. Relaxation produces alpha brain wave patterns that activate your right brain — the creative, intuitive side. You can practice visualization when you first wake up in the morning as a way to set the tone for the day or before you go to sleep as a great way to end the day. Alternate Nostril Breathing as described in the training section on page 72 is an effective way to get into a state of relaxation.

I like to use visualization before an important business meeting or event. I imagine how I would like to see it all play out in my mind. Then I take action in my physical reality. It often turns out the way I imagined or even better. It's important to let go of attachment to the outcome. This way you can be pleasantly surprised without being disappointed.

AWARENESS EXERCISE

Visualization inspires you to take action. If you are not producing the desired results you want then you need to ask "what have I not been willing to do?" Sometimes you have to be willing to let go of the fear and doubt that stands in your way and blocks your dreams and desires. A release of fear can free you to take the next action step.

ACTION STEPS

1) Practice visualization daily to use the creativity of your mind in a powerful way.

2) To reinforce visualization, I encourage you to make a vision board. This is a fun technique that is an extremely powerful tool for manifesting. Simply cut out pictures and words from magazines, etc., that represent what you want. Arrange them on a poster board or in a scrapbook and look at them every day to stimulate your creative mind.

EXPAND

Everything you desire has a feeling associated with it. When you expand your mind to get to the feeling, you will be in harmony with what you want. This is the BE—DO—HAVE principle. When you become the feeling, then you naturally will do what is necessary to have what you desire. For example, if the feeling associated with having a healthy, fit body is confidence, then you can use visualization to generate that feeling. It is that feeling of confidence that will help you do whatever it takes to have the health and fitness

you desire. When you feel loving, you attract loving relationships. When you feel generous, you attract wealth. When you feel confident, you attract opportunities. In other words, good feelings attract good things into your life. Your thoughts and feelings are magnetic energy. It's the Law of Attraction.

Remember, where your attention goes, energy flows. Put your attention on what you want to see in your life with the power of visualization, get to the feeling that goes with it and watch what happens. You will be amazed at how your dreams and desires begin to appear — like magic!

AWARENESS EXERCISE

Write an example of how your positive energy attracted what you wanted in your life.

ACTION STEPS

Whenever you visualize what you want, write it down, and always get to the feeling that is associated with having it. Keep a written account of what you attract and manifest in your life.

FOCUS

Focus is power. It is the difference between the intensity of an ordinary light bulb and the power of a laser beam. The mind has been likened to a drunken monkey, constantly leaping from one thing to another. In order to master the monkey, you have to train it to be still. A calm mind is a focused mind. Without focus, all of your efforts lack effectiveness. Use the power of conscious breathing to stay calm and present in each moment of your life. Focus on the positive feelings that raise your energy vibrations to a higher level of positive attraction.

When you are fully awake and concentrating your attention in the present moment, you have the power to create without the limitations of your ego. The ego dwells in past and future thinking and operates from fear. Your conscious self lives in the unlimited potential of each and every moment.

Use your imagination to focus on what you intend to manifest. As a drowning man wants air, you must focus on what you desire. This intensity of concentration will get rid of obstacles that try to divert your attention. Always use the power of intention for the highest good of all concerned. To be clear about that, add this statement to what you ask for:

"This or something better now manifests for the highest good of all concerned."

Let go of any attachment to the outcome. The primary objective of mental discipline is to train your mind to:

- Focus on being in the present moment.
- Imagine what you want rather than what you don't want.
- Raise your energy vibrations with positive thoughts.

AWARENESS EXERCISE

- Notice when your mind is focused on past or future thinking. When you're aware of it, make a conscious choice to connect with your body and return to the present moment where life is happening.
- Observe how you feel when you focus on having what you don't want.
- Be aware of how you feel when you focus on having what you do want.

ACTION STEPS

Practice conscious breathing as a way to stay connected with your body and focused in the present moment.

When you practice visualization always get to the feeling you associate with having what you desire. For example, if confidence is what you would feel if you were healthy and fit, then get to that feeling by imagining yourself being healthy and fit. Reinforce this image with a mantra (instrument of the mind), i.e., "I am healthy and fit."

"Every moment of your life is infinitely creative and the Universe is endlessly bountiful. Just put forth a clear enough request, and everything your heart desires must come to you."
- Shakti Gawain, Author

EMOTIONAL HARMONY

Emotions are the language of the soul. They are the way your soul communicates with you to get your attention. Your emotions let you know if you are operating on a track of love or a track of fear. All of your unpleasant, painful emotions come from fear, and all of your pleasant, uplifting emotions come from love. If you ignore your feelings, you will be ignoring valuable information that is meant to guide you out of fear (painful feelings) and back to love (good feelings).

For example, if you put your hand on a hot stove, you want to feel the pain. It's telling you something. "Move your hand!" That's a loving response to pain. If you didn't pay attention to the pain and left your hand there, you would suffer much more. The same holds true for emotional pain. If you pay attention, get the message, and take care of yourself, you are responding with love. Then the pain goes away.

Emotion = Energy + Motion. This is energy that needs to move. Our emotions are what move us to take action. Do you want your actions to be motivated by love or by fear?

"All you need is love."
- The Beatles

Emotional harmony starts by honoring your deepest feelings. What you experience in life gets stored in cell memory and in your energy field. This energy field extends beyond the physical body approximately an arm's distance all around you. It is an electrical system that gives and receives messages to and from other people. All of your life experiences have created the physical and emotional energy bodies you now occupy.

The human energy system has within it seven power centers or vortexes known as chakras that run from the base of the spine to the crown of the head. We receive information from these centers to help us understand what we are experiencing.

Chakras, in Hindu metaphysical tradition, are centers of Prana or life force energy. Corresponding to vital points in the body, the name is derived from the Sanskrit word for "wheel." In yogic context, the word "vortex" comes to mind. Chakras appear as spinning wheels of energy that turn rapidly in a clockwise direction when the body is young and vital.

Your chakra system is like the instrument panel in your car. If you pay attention to the gauges that provide information about the gas, oil, battery, water, etc., and notice the speed you are traveling, you are more likely to enjoy the journey without breaking down or getting a ticket.

To understand the information being transmitted from the chakras, you need to become aware of their connection to a particular part of the body, the life lessons to which they relate, and the colors associated with each which offer clues to what you are experiencing.

1st Chakra — ROOT

Location: Base of the spine

Color: Red

Life Lessons: Survival, family of origin, connection to the earth, primal power

2nd Chakra — SACRAL

Location: Two inches below the navel

Color: Orange

Life Lessons: Creativity, exploration, sexuality, work, money, relationships

3rd Chakra — SOLAR PLEXUS

Location: Center point beneath the rib cage

Color: Yellow

Life Lessons: Personal power, integrity, self-esteem, personality, intellect, perception

4th Chakra — HEART

Location: Center of the chest

Color: Green

Life Lessons: Love, compassion, forgiveness, kindness, connection, growth

5th Chakra — THROAT

Location: Center of the throat

Color: Blue

Life Lessons: Communication, emotional expression, clarification, expression

6th Chakra—BROW (Third Eye)

Location: Slightly above and between the eyebrows

Color: Indigo

Life Lessons: Intuition, insight, vision, depth

7th Chakra—CROWN

Location: Top of the head in the center

Color: Violet

Life Lessons: Spirituality, wisdom, guidance, awareness, being

AWARENESS EXERCISE

Become familiar with your seven energy centers and where they are located.

AWARENESS

In order to keep loving energy flowing through you, you have to be aware of when you are blocking it with fear. Love is the energy that comes from your heart. It is the essence of who you are, and all the positive feelings generated by love, translate into loving behavior. Fear, on the other hand, is felt as negative feelings that come from an insecure ego. FEAR is an acronym for: False Expectations Appearing Real. Fear contracts and love expands. This is the underlying difference between positive and negative emotions. Positive energy expands and attracts. Negative energy contracts and repels.

"When we really love ourselves, everything in our life works." - Louise L. Hay

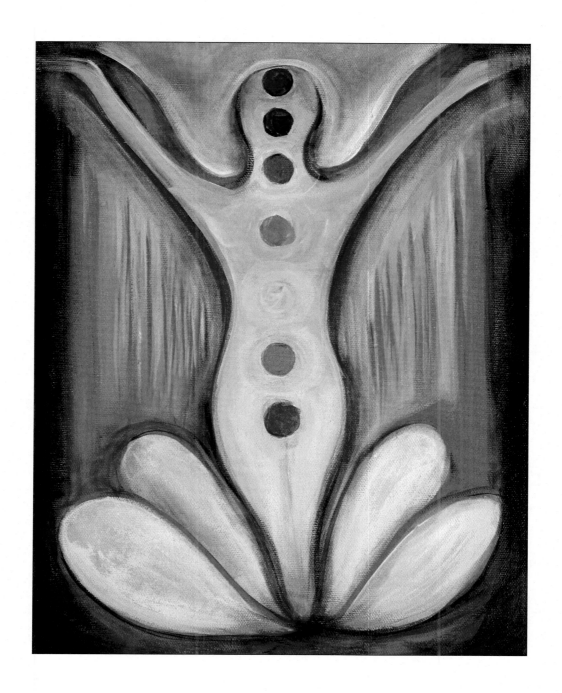

When you feel bad, your ego is running the show. By observing the ego operating out of fear, you can disassociate from this aspect of the mind and become conscious. Your conscious higher self can take over and choose to respond from love. All negative feelings have a message. Once you get the message, the feeling can move on. Most of us have repressed so many of these feelings that they have gotten stuck in our bodies as emotional tension that needs to be released.

Emotion is dynamic energy that needs to move. The Tibetan lamas have an ancient secret to the fountain of youth that they have been practicing for generations called the Five Tibetan Rites (see page 72). These yoga-like movements restore health and vitality by stimulating and toning the energy vortexes (chakras). When you practice these exercises daily you not only develop an awareness of emotional energy, you also increase vitality and reverse aging.

Your seven energy centers govern the seven ductless glands in the body's endocrine system, which regulate all of the body's functions, including the aging process. When we are young and healthy our chakras spin at great speed. This spinning allows vital life force energy to move upward through the endocrine system (reproductive, adrenals, pancreas, thymus, thyroid, pituitary and pineal). If these vortexes slow down or get blocked, illness and aging occur. The Five Rites keep the chakras spinning at a rapid rate for optimal health and well-being.

AWARENESS EXERCISE
Get into a comfortable position with your spine straight, close your eyes and bring your attention to your heart center in the center of your chest. Use your breath to help you connect. Notice what you feel, physically and emotionally.

ACTION STEPS
Practice identifying your emotions. Once you identify what you're feeling, ask "what is the message?" For example, let's say the emotion is anger. The message could be that you need to stop holding back and speak up for yourself. If you do this in a loving way, it will be a productive use of that energy.

When you feel sad, be aware of what you are thinking that is causing an unpleasant emotion. Allow yourself to feel what you are feeling and get the message. Once you have the message, you can change your thoughts and your emotions will change automatically.

RELEASING
We come into this world knowing how to release our emotions. Crying and laughter are two good examples of how we let go of intense emotional

"If you want to find the secrets of the Universe, think in terms of energy, frequency, and vibration." - Nikola Tesla

44

energy. Have you ever tried to suppress tears or laughter? The effort is draining. Crying is the body's natural way of releasing emotional pain. Tears of sadness actually contain toxins that the body needs to get rid of, and they have a different chemical composition than tears of joy. When we allow complete emotional release, we feel cleansed. Stuffing negative feelings can cause a continual chemical release that eventually causes an imbalance. This can lead to more pain, illness and dis-ease. Remember, E-motion is Energy + Motion. It's energy that needs to move.

When we pay attention to the signals we get throughout the day, whether they take the form of a headache, backache, depression, anxiety, etc., we have the opportunity to get the message. This is how to get to the root cause of pain rather than just deal with the symptoms. Our culture has taught us to rely on a multitude of distractions to get rid of pain. We learn to cover up uncomfortable feelings with drugs, food, alcohol, sex, work, television, internet surfing, or anything that serves as a distraction from unpleasant emotions.

The body is a physical picture of our thoughts. Emotions are the energy that hold our thoughts together to form the picture. Mental release comes when you identify the feeling and get the message. Emotional release comes from letting go of negative energy and taking care of our needs.

You can release the energy of repressed negative emotions with deep breathing and exercise. The spinal rock, a yoga movement that massages the entire spine, can be performed with deep exhalations to facilitate letting go of emotional tension before it becomes distress. You will learn this exercise in the next section (see page 75). If you need more release, a good primal scream into a pillow or in your car with the windows up is also effective.

AWARENESS EXERCISE

Pay attention to your second chakra located about two inches below your navel. Breathe into this energy center for 10 breaths and imagine the color orange filling your belly. Ask: "What do I need to let go of?"

ACTION STEPS

To release emotional tension practice:

- Deep, heavy sighing
- Screaming into a pillow
- Dancing and moving your hips
- Sports such as tennis, golf, volleyball, or racquetball. Grunt if you feel like it.
- Laughing at a comedy for no reason other than it feels good.

ENHANCING

Enhance a feeling and it completes itself. It moves us to tears, laughter, or action. Our emotions are what make life interesting. Can you imagine a world without passion? Passion is intense emotional energy that needs to have an outlet for expression. Resistance to any part of the human experience, especially our emotions, limits our potential as creative beings. By enhancing our feelings, we can dive into the depths of our emotional well, and surface with the loving energy we need to express them in a healthy way.

Feelings are as much a part of who you are as your height, weight, eye and hair color. Can you describe your emotional self as easily as your physical self? A typical greeting we have for one another is "how are you?" A common response is "fine thank you, how are you?" Does "fine" describe how you feel or is it a general term for not being aware of your emotional state?

The deeper you breathe, the better you feel. Take a deep cleansing breath right now. Visualize a clear stream of water coming up from the earth into the base of your spine, up to the crown of the head and back down the spine like a waterfall into the earth. This kind of breathing is very cleansing and enhances emotional energy. You can literally change the way you feel just by changing the way you breathe. Shallow breathing is constrictive. Deep breathing is expansive.

You can enhance neutral or positive feelings with your vocabulary. If someone asks how you are and you automatically say "fine" or "okay," you can take yourself up a notch by responding with "I'm good." If you're inclined to respond with "good" then you can enhance that emotional

state by saying "I'm great...wonderful...excellent... fantastic!" Observe how it enhances the way you feel when you increase your enthusiasm with words.

Your posture and tone of voice also influence the way you feel. Notice the difference in how you feel simply by standing or sitting with your spine straight, projecting from your diaphragm and expressing from your heart.

AWARENESS EXERCISE

How are you today? Be aware of your response now and whenever you are asked that question. Practice taking it to the next level and notice the affect it has on you and the person asking the question.

ACTION STEPS

When you want to enhance the way you feel, use these four techniques:

1. Take several deep cleansing breaths.
2. Words are powerful. Step it up a notch with words that go beyond your present state. For example, when you feel good, say "I feel great!"
3. Your posture is body language. If you want to feel better, adjust your posture to lengthen your spine and relax your shoulders.
4. Breathe from your diaphragm when you speak and you will feel more powerful.

EXPRESSION

Once you have become aware of what you're

feeling, gotten the message, released negative emotions, and feel more relaxed, then it's possible to return to your natural state of well-being. This is an excellent opportunity to connect heart-to-heart with others and communicate from a place of emotional harmony.

Creative forms of expression provide healthy outlets for emotional energy. It is also useful to channel positive energy into being creative. Writing, dancing, singing, playing an instrument, painting, drawing, interior decorating, photography, cooking, etc., are activities that get your creative juices flowing and channel emotional energy.

Stream of consciousness writing is useful when you want to explore your feelings and emotions more deeply. You can start with "I feel . . ." then start writing whatever comes to mind. This form of self-expression can be very enlightening and liberating for your heart and soul.

Love is the way to self-realization—it is the essence of who you really are. When you get off track and get stuck in the fears of the ego, your soul will let you know. You are like a pilot that has set a course for love. The plane continually strays off course and it's up to you, the pilot, to keep directing it back on course. Emotions connect you with your soul. You need emotions to feel your way back to your natural state of harmony.

Emotional harmony occurs when your body,

mind, heart and spirit are in alignment. You have to be tuned in to know when you are out of alignment. Negative beliefs about yourself are the primary source of fear. Fear stops your natural loving energy from flowing freely.

Examine your erroneous beliefs and you will discover that they are preventing you from living and loving fully. Let go of negative beliefs that were formed in your early childhood and you will transform your life.

AWARENESS EXERCISE
1) What are your negative beliefs about yourself?

2) Are you willing to let go of these beliefs? Y/N

3) What are your positive beliefs about yourself?

4) How can you strengthen these beliefs?

ACTION STEPS
1. Track your fears to your negative beliefs.

Example: Fear of public speaking

Beliefs:

- I'm not good enough.
- I will be punished if they don't like what I say.
- I have to do it perfectly to be accepted.
- I might say something stupid and feel humiliated.

2. Create new beliefs.

Example:

- I am good enough.
- I'll be okay no matter what happens.
- I intend to do my best and that's good enough.

Act as if the new beliefs are true. Your actions will strengthen the new belief and the old ones will lose their power over you.

EMOTIONAL ENERGY PROCESS (EEP)

This is a life-changing process to uncover limiting beliefs that operate at a subconscious level and change them at a conscious level.

1) Pay attention to your negative emotion.

2) Be aware of your thoughts.

3) Ask yourself, "What kind of belief would I need to have about myself to have these thoughts?" (Remember this belief is subconscious and was formed in your childhood)

4) Ask, "Do I want to change this belief?" To what?

5) Now what do I think about what happened when I come from this new belief?

6) Is there a new feeling associated with these thoughts?

7) The best time to reinforce your new beliefs is when you first wake up in the morning before the mind chatter begins.

With this process your ego has been alerted that your intention is to change a limiting belief to an empowering belief and that you are looking for evidence to reinforce the new belief in your life.

SPIRITUAL FREEDOM

There are two lifestyles to choose from — natural or normal. You either have a life that is directed by your soul or ruled by your ego. Most of us live a combination of both. Normal living is based on external influences. It's the kind of existence we fall into when we don't realize we have a choice. If we're taught from childhood that life is about achieving for the purpose of acquiring material wealth and recognition, we tend to head in that direction. We pursue grades, degrees, jobs, cars, houses, and material possessions. Then we have children who perpetuate the cycle.

This can be a great life for those who are content with the never ending pursuit of doing and having more. In fact, it is widely accepted, respected, and expected by those who conform to what's normal. The problem with this way of life is that the ego is never satisfied, and the soul longs for greater joy and fulfillment.

What happens if you lose the things that define you in the material world? Who are you then?

That is the risk attached to achieving for the purpose of having more and being recognized for what you have acquired. Even some of our television game shows demonstrate this behavior of risking everything in the pursuit of having more. The achiever in the game of life may have to risk the loss of health, relationships, peace of mind, and personal fulfillment for the sake of acquiring more material wealth. It is a risk that many people are willing to take when caught up in the whirlwind of endless pursuit. Unfortunately there is never enough material wealth to fill the void of feeling empty on the inside. True wealth, the kind you can't lose, comes from within. Once we are in touch with our interior space, then material wealth can be an added blessing with lessons in gratitude.

When you discipline the ego to cooperate with your soul, you are free to receive spiritual guidance. Guidance comes through intuition — a powerful feeling, a sign, an unexpected flash of insight, or a realization during or after meditation. The challenge is learning to trust your intuition enough to follow it, even when your ego has a different opinion. Spiritual freedom is being conscious enough to observe the ego and not allow it to run your life.

Acceptance, Trust, Gratitude and Unconditional Love are the connecting links that will align your body, mind, heart and spirit in their natural state of freedom. These are the qualities that come with stillness. The Western mind doesn't see much value in sitting still and doing nothing, so we give it a reason to be still. In the stillness you have access to spiritual guidance that makes your life more fulfilling and less stressful. It connects you with a higher source of wisdom that takes decision-making to a whole new level.

By consciously tuning into the frequency of pure love, you will remember who you really are at the core of your being. You are like a radio that is always plugged in, however, it's up to you to turn on the radio, tune in to the right frequency, and listen. Inner silence allows you to hear the message that's being transmitted to help guide you on your journey through life.

Your breath connects you with your spirit. When you imagine the light and love of your spiritual self as energy you breathe into your body, you will make a conscious connection to your higher power. This spiritual energy will fill your body, mind and heart to the point where love is all you have inside of you. What happens when you squeeze an orange? You get orange juice. What happens when you get squeezed with the pressures of life? What comes out of you? If love is all you have inside of you, then love is all that will come out of you.

Acknowledging your spirituality is like having a card to an infinite library of wisdom. To activate the card all you have to do is be willing to use it to expand your life experience. Know that we are all connected to the same source of universal intelligence.

AWARENESS EXERCISE

How often do you enjoy inner silence?

Daily ___ Weekly ___ Sometimes ___
Rarely ___ Never ___

Do you feel connected to your spirit? Y/N

ACTION STEPS

Set aside at least ten minutes a day to enjoy inner silence. This can be practiced with eyes open or closed. Let your body be still as you focus your attention on your breathing and quiet the chatter in your mind. Be aware of your body. Observe your thoughts. Pay attention to your feelings. This is an excellent way to connect with your spirit, the greater part of yourself that is aware of the physical, mental, and emotional aspects.

Keep a journal of your insights and observations.

ACCEPTANCE

Spiritual freedom begins with acceptance of yourself as a spiritual being having a human experience. Seeing yourself from this perspective, opens up a whole new way to live your life. Rather than thinking of yourself as a human being who occasionally has spiritual experiences, you realize that your soul is on a journey of evolution which includes the human experience. From this perspective you have unlimited potential.

Accept your physical body as the vehicle for your soul's journey. Have a loving, respectful relationship with your body. Take care of it so it will run at optimum performance for a lifetime. Most people take better care of their cars than they do their own bodies. Your body, like your car, will run much better if properly maintained. When you are critical or abusive of your body, it is a sign that you are not accepting and respecting it. Once you make the shift towards loving and cherishing your body, you will give it what it needs to be healthy and fit.

Your life is a gift, even the parts of it that you find challenging. To accept all of it frees you from the struggle and stress of resistance to what is. When life presents challenges, it is an opportunity to learn, grow, and evolve. You are much more than any of your problems. Perceiving "problems" as "opportunities" frees you to respond to challenges in a positive way.

In addition to accepting oneself, acceptance of others is a life-changing, spiritual practice. Everyone, including you, is doing the best they know how. When you catch yourself judging someone, ask yourself: "What is the positive intention behind his or her behavior?"

There is a positive intention behind a negative

behavior because everyone's ego is always trying to feel better. Even the act of judging is a way for the ego to feel superior. When you let go of your judgments you let go of your ego's need to feel superior — an important aspect of personal freedom.

AWARENESS EXERCISE

Think of someone you have a hard time accepting. Look at the behavior you dislike most and see if you can find the positive intention behind it.

Behavior:

Judgment:

Positive Intention:

ACTION STEPS

Connect with your spirit every day.

1) Spend time communing with nature.

2) Enjoy inner silence / meditate.

3) Breathe deeply.

4) Accept your life and learn from the challenges.

5) Let go of the need to judge.

TRUST

When someone does something to lose our trust, we expect them to earn it back with their actions. Can you imagine how your soul feels every time it sends you a message through intuition and you don't trust it enough to follow through with your actions? You may have to earn the trust of your soul to strengthen your intuition. Pay attention to your spiritual guidance by acting on it and it will steer you in the right direction. The more you trust it, the more it will trust you to take the right action.

If you have trust issues with others, a good place to start resolving those issues is with yourself. It's difficult to trust others when you can't trust yourself. Perhaps you don't trust yourself because you've been listening to your ego more than your soul. Your intuition is an inner knowing. It can show up as a gut feeling, a heart sensation, chills running up and down your spine, or the hairs standing up on the back of your neck.

The higher your self-esteem, the stronger your intuition will be. For example, if your intuition is telling you to leave an unhealthy situation and you do it even though it's difficult, your self-esteem will increase. It takes courage to face your fears, and courage is the backbone of self-esteem.

AWARENESS EXERCISE

1) Describe a situation when you didn't trust your intuition enough to follow it:

What was the outcome?

2) Describe a situation when you did trust your your intuition enough to follow it:

What was the outcome?

ACTION STEPS

- Practice listening to your intuition and following through with action.
- Keep a journal of your experiences.

GRATITUDE

There is always so much to be grateful for even when everything isn't the way you'd like it to be. Be grateful for spiritual guidance. Notice the many gifts in your life and express gratitude for whatever you feel thankful for in each moment. Simply shifting your focus to one of gratitude will bring peace to you in the present moment.

In this country, we devote one day a year to being grateful. We call it Thanksgiving. Why not be be grateful for at least one thing each day? Focus on strengthening this particular spiritual muscle. You might want to give the day a theme like, "I am grateful for my body." You could give it 10 minutes or devote an entire day to pampering your body. Go for a walk in nature, enjoy a delicious meal, listen to your favorite music, get a massage, practice yoga, relax in a bath by candlelight, or engage in any activity or non-activity that will make your body feel appreciated. Even just buying fresh flowers is a way of honoring your body. Appreciation is so uplifting. Why not make it a practice every day of your life?

Expressing gratitude is not just saying "thank you." It's also about giving back — to yourself, your family, friends, community, and the world. It is the attitude that leads to unconditional love. As I mentioned before, since what you focus on expands, if you focus on what you are grateful for every day, you will see more of that in your life.

AWARENESS EXERCISE

Name five five things for which you are grateful:
1.
2.
3.
4.
5.

ACTION STEPS

- Express gratitude to someone every day.
- Share what you have with others, even if it's simply a smile or a kind word.
- Identify three things you appreciate about yourself:

1.
2.
3.

UNCONDITIONAL LOVE

It's easy to love yourself when you're doing everything perfectly. It's easy to love others when they're behaving the way you want. Unconditional love is total acceptance without attachments or expectations. Choose to give love for the pure joy of expressing who you really are.

Compassion and forgiveness are two essential components of unconditional love. Compassion moves you from your head to your heart. When you care about another person and want to be of service, you are connecting soul-to-soul. One act of compassion will free you from the illusion that you are separate. What you give to others, you ultimately give to yourself.

To forgive is to let go of the judgment that your past should have been different than what it was. Forgiveness benefits the one doing the forgiving as much, if not more than the one being forgiven. It doesn't mean that you accept being treated badly. It means you take responsibility for your life experiences. To blame others for what happens gives them power over you. You become a puppet who allows others to pull the strings that determine your emotions and behavior.

As spiritual beings having a human experience, we are actually leading double lives. Our spirit exists in a state of freedom where everything is connected through pure love. Simultaneously, the body-mind lives in a world of separation that is dominated by the ego. The challenge is to bring the pure love of your spirit into each moment of your life. Let your soul be your guide with your ego as a companion for survival in the physical world. This is the way to create peace and harmony in your life.

Spiritual freedom awakens your ability to love yourself and others unconditionally. As you connect with this energy resource, you will discover what a magnificent being you really are. This will allow you to see the light and love inherent in every human being.

AWARENESS EXERCISE

Do you love yourself unconditionally?
Do you love others unconditionally?
Are you compassionate?
Are you able to forgive and let go of resentment?

ACTION STEPS

- Practice unconditional love for yourself by realizing that you are always doing the best you know how.

Practice unconditional love for others by acknowledging that they are doing the best they know how.

SATORI YOGA™

Satori Yoga™ consists of four distinct parts: Energetics for physical balance, Masterminding for mental wholeness, Emotionalizing for emotional harmony, and Innercises for spiritual freedom to restore energy , create awareness and deepen the connection to your body, mind, heart, and spirit.

BALANCE

When we resist what is happening in the present moment, tension builds and upsets our natural balance. *Energetics* helps restore balance by releasing the physical tension caused by stress. Relaxation is our natural state. We are either creating ease or dis-ease by the way we respond to life.

WHOLENESS

Masterminding is the art of training your mind to master your thoughts. By combining your male and female energies to work together, a sense of wholeness is created. When you realize that you have the wisdom to be creative (feminine energy) and the power to manifest what you imagine (masculine energy), you operate from a place of wholeness.

HARMONY

Emotionalizing helps you stay on a course of love. When you get off course and operate from fear, your emotions let you know. You can always restore harmony by making the choice to return to love. When your thoughts, feelings and actions are aligned with your highest good, you are in harmony and that feels good.

FREEDOM

Innercises lead to freedom. This discipline helps you turn inward into the silence and connect with the source of your being. This expansive state of awareness takes you out of your ego, and frees your soul to be happy and content. To be fully present in each moment, no matter what is happening, is true freedom.

ENERGETICS

You can practice *Energetics* first thing in the morning to get your energy moving or later in the day to release tension and increase energy.

- Breathing exercises increase endurance.
- Yoga creates flexibility.
- Self-massage adds strength.
- Deep relaxation provides calm, soothing energy.

The entire sequence takes approximately 40 minutes to complete. It is best to do these exercises in a quiet place free of interruptions. Although practicing all four components together is the most effective way to restore balance, feel free to use any of the four components separately if you only have five or ten minutes for a quick energy boost. Even if you only practice one of the four parts every day, you will experience an increase in your energy level. *Energetics* is also a great way to prepare for more vigorous exercise because it warms you up and promotes circulation.

BREATHING EXERCISES

These seven exercises will increase your lung capacity by filling them with energy-boosting oxygen. If you feel lightheaded while performing these exercises, do fewer repetitions and rest briefly between sets. All breathing exercises require that you breathe in through your nose and out through your mouth except for Core Breath where you will do just the opposite.

1) Core Breath

Place your hands on the lower part of your rib cage and give this area a massage to increase blood flow. Keep your hands on your ribs as you breathe in through pursed lips as though you are inhaling through a straw.

Feel the rib cage expand as you breathe in. As you exhale through your nose, concentrate on contracting the inner rib cage muscles and pull the ribs together. Do four repetitions.

2) Standing Breath

Stand straight with feet shoulder-width apart, shoulders relaxed. Breathe in through your nose to the count of six as you raise your arms up and overhead, and look up. Hold your breath for four counts, then breathe out to the count of six as you slowly lower your arms down to your sides. Do four repetitions.

3) Opening Breath

Stand with your feet shoulder-width apart. Lace your fingers together and place your knuckles under your chin. Inhale slowly to the count of six feeling the air moving at the back of your throat. Raise your elbows up towards your ears while pressing down with your chin against your hands. Let your head drop back and exhale through your mouth bringing your elbows together slowly in front. Bring your head forward, press your chin down, and begin another cycle. Do eight repetitions.

1)

2)

3)

4) Balancing Breath

Stand with your feet about two feet apart. As you inhale, bring your arms up with elbows bent and hands making tight fists. As you exhale, squat down while pulling your elbows down. Inhale as you straighten your left leg and balance while you lift your right knee and left arm up. Go back to squatting position, exhaling. Inhale as you switch to standing on your right leg.

5) Stretching Breath

Stand with feet wide apart. Breathe in through your nose and as you exhale, squat down, arms bent in front with tight fists. Contract abdominal muscles as you breathe out completely through your mouth. As you inhale, straighten up and stretch your arms up, and bend to the right. Breathe out as you squat. Breathe in and stretch to the left. Do eight repetitions.

6) Swinging Breath

Stand with your feet wide apart. Swing your arms up and to one side as you breathe in. As you squat down, exhale, circle arms in front, and then swing your arms up to the other side and inhale. Do eight repetitions.

4)

5)

7) Bowing Breath

Stand with feet hip-distance apart. Begin with arms down in front, palms together. As you breathe in, bring your hands behind your neck, tighten your buttocks to protect your lower back, and arch back gently by pushing your hips forward (you can bend your knees slightly if you wish) for a good stretch. Hold your breath for a moment. Now bring your arms and body forward with knees bent, and swing your arms back as you exhale completely through your mouth. Then inhale through your nose, swing your arms up and repeat the movement. Do eight repetitions.

YOGA WARM-UP

Warm up your neck and shoulders before doing the yoga sequence. Breathe in and out through your nose feeling the air move in the back of your throat as though you were silently saying "haaa." Breathe in as you go into the stretch, and breathe out as you focus on letting go of tension.

Neck Stretch

Bring your head towards your right shoulder and breathe out the tension. Come back to center. Bring your head towards your left shoulder and breathe out the tension there. Return to center.

Shoulder Rolls

As you breathe in, raise your shoulders up, and then roll them back and down as you breathe out. Do this four times. Now reverse the movement. Raise your shoulders up, forward and down. Do this four more times.

YOGA
Salutation to the Full Moon

Dedicate this series to the ending of a cycle and letting go of what you don't need.

Stand with feet apart and hands together at the center of your chest. Raise arms up, clasp one hand around the opposite wrist and pull gently as you bend to one side. Return to center and repeat on the other side. Return to center. Reach up with your hands, then look up and arch your back gently keeping your buttocks engaged. Come back to center. Bend forward hinging from the hips, knees slightly bent. With a flat back, lower your hands towards your feet. Relax your arms, neck, and shoulders to the count of five. Reverse that move lifting your arms out to the side. Stand up straight with hands overhead.

Step or jump your feet apart about three feet, arms reaching out to the side, palms down. Turn your right foot out and back foot slightly inward. Bend your right knee so that it is directly over your right ankle. Place your right forearm on your right thigh, extend your left arm straight up from the shoulder, palm facing forward. Bend from the waist. Hold briefly and breathe. Make sure your hips are open. If you feel steady, look up at your left hand and hold briefly. Another more advanced version is to bring your right hand down in front of your ankle. Return to center and repeat on the left side.

Come up and turn towards the left leg. Bring your arms behind your waist with hands clasping your arms or elbows. Lower your chin towards your chest. Then lower your forehead down towards your left knee. Keep your forward leg straight (you may bend it slightly if you need to). Relax your neck and shoulders. Breathe and focus on one point to keep your balance. Return to center. Turn the opposite direction and repeat on the right side.

Both feet face forward, then jump or step together and bring your arms straight up touching your palms together. Lower hands down in front, palms together. Place the back of your hands together and breathe in deeply as you bring your hands up the center of your body until they reach overhead again. Breathe out slowly as you lower your arms down by your sides and bring palms together at the center of your chest. Do the entire sequence one more time, and notice your body letting go of tension as it becomes more flexible.

Salutation to the New Moon

Dedicate this series to the beginning of a cycle and what you want to bring into your life.

Stand with your feet together, hands at heart center. Raise your arms up and clasp your hands together with index fingers pointing up. Bend to one side, hold briefly and breathe. Come back to center and repeat on the other side. Return to center. Look up, tighten your buttocks to protect your lower back and arch back gently. Come back to center.

With knees slightly bent, bend forward hinging from the hips. With a flat back, lower your hands towards your feet. Relax your arms, neck, and shoulders to the count of five. Reverse that move lifting your arms out to the side. Stand up straight with your hands overhead and touching.

Step or jump your feet about three feet apart, arms reaching out to the side, palms down. Turn your right foot out and back foot slightly inward. Keep your right leg straight and reach out with your right hand, looking at your middle finger. Lower your right hand to your calf or ankle and extend your left arm up, palms facing forward. Hold and breathe. Imagine a string connected to your left hand pulling you up, and return to center. Repeat on the other side.

Come up and turn towards your left leg. Bring the right leg back and balance on the ball of your foot in a lunge position. Bring your arms overhead and arch back gently. Return to center. Turn to the other side and repeat.

With feet facing forward, jump or step together and bring your arms overhead. Lower your hands down in front, palms together. Turn the back of your hands together and as you breathe deeply, bring your hands up the center of your body, and reach overhead. Breathe out slowly as you lower your arms down to your sides and bring your hands together at the center of your chest. Repeat this entire sequence one more time.

NOTE: Read through the instructions on this page and follow the illustrations through to page 66.

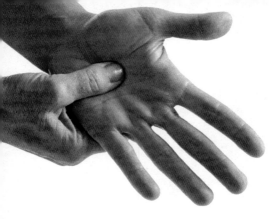

Self Massage

This massage incorporates reflexology and acupressure points to stimulate energy flow throughout the body. As you massage your body to stimulate the flow of energy and release tension, remember to breathe deeply and concentrate on the way your body feels.

Reflexology

Use your right thumb to massage the palm of your left hand. Using the thumb and forefinger, start at the base of each finger and massage toward the tip. Squeeze the tip firmly. Then shake out the hand that is doing the massage.

For headache relief, press your right thumb into the web between your left thumb and first finger, gripping it firmly for eight seconds. Repeat entire massage on the other hand. Shake hands out vigorously.

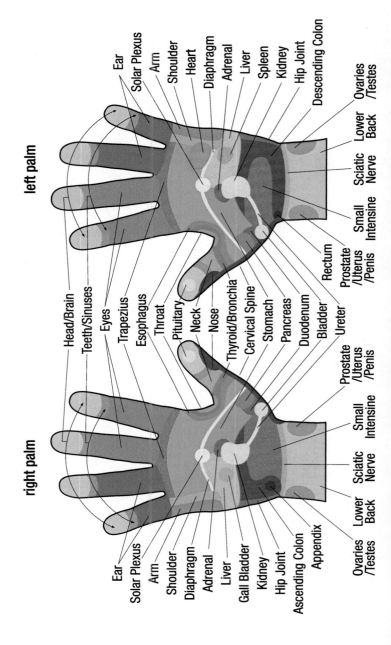

This massage can also be done on the feet.

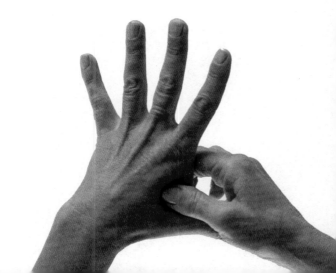

Strengthen Abdominal Muscles

Place your fingertips on the top of your head, thumbs to the side. Press and pull the scalp apart. Do this five times with pressure.

Relieve Mental Strain

Using the palms of your hands, massage your temples in a circular motion going forward with medium pressure.

Relieve Mental & Emotional Tension

Place your thumb and middle finger on your forehead above the center of each eyebrow, halfway between your eyebrows and hair line. Touch lightly.

Strengthen Muscles in the Front and Release Tension in the Back of the Neck

Place fingertips on either side of your spine at the base of the scull in the two pockets and massage firmly in a circular motion.

Increase Circulation (1 & 2)

Lower your head toward the right shoulder and let it move forward slightly. Place the fingertips of your right hand on the left side of your neck and massage down the side of your neck and along the upper back until you reach your shoulder. Concentrate on knots or sore spots and breathe deeply as you massage. Take your time. Squeeze your shoulder and continue down your left arm to the wrist. Repeat on the other side.

Strengthen the Upper Back (3) (supraspinatus)

Bring your right thumb to the top of your left shoulder joint resting your other four fingers in your armpit. With a downward stroke from top to bottom, massage these points five times. Repeat on the other side.

Stimulate the Lymphatic System and Eliminate Toxins (4)

Place your fingertips on your chest in front of your armpit and massage in a circular motion. Repeat on the other side.

Strengthen Thigh (5) Muscles (quadriceps)

Center the fingertips of both hands underneath the curve of your ribcage. Massage under the curve to the bottom of the ribcage. Do this five times.

Strengthen Backs of the Legs (6) (Hamstrings)

Bring fingertips of both hands on the front of your hip bones to align your thumbs to the back on top of the most prominent bones on either side of your low back. Massage firmly.

Strengthen Shoulders (7) (Deltoids)

While standing straight with your arms down by your sides where your fingertips touch the side of your outer thighs, massage those points firmly.

Shake hands out vigorously to relax them. Lace fingers together and stretch your arms over your head, palms up. Bring hands down together in front and squeeze them.

DEEP RELAXATION

Once you have released physical tension through breathing, yoga, and self-massage, it will be easier to enter a state of deep relaxation.

Lay flat on your back so your spine is straight, feet resting comfortably apart with arms down by your sides away from your body, palms facing up. Or you may sit on a chair with your feet on the floor. The best mental state to be in is one of surrender. Let go of thoughts about the past or future, surrender to the present moment, and connect with the wisdom of your body.

Progressive Relaxation

Flex your feet towards your head, tighten your calves, knees, and thighs; then let the all tightness go. Tighten your buttocks; then release those muscles. Contract your abdominal muscles; then relax. Press your chest up slightly towards the ceiling; then relax. Make tight fists with both hands and squeeze your arms into a tight biceps curl; then release them. Raise your shoulders up towards your ears; then drop them down. Tighten all the muscles in your face, squeeze your eyes, mouth, and forehead; then relax those muscles. Finally, take a deep breath, expanding your abdomen, diaphragm, and chest. Hold for a moment; then exhale and release all the tension left in your body.

Autogenics

Give yourself the following suggestions:

Allow your right leg to feel heavy. Left leg heavy. Right arm heavy. Left arm heavy. Bring your awareness to your solar plexus (in the center of your body beneath your ribcage). Suggest that this area feels warm and comfortable. Focus your attention on the center of your forehead. Suggest that it feels cool and calm.

Imagery

Imagine yourself resting in a peaceful place in nature. Be aware of your surroundings. Connect with this place as your private sanctuary where you can always go to be at peace. Allow the tranquility of your environment to permeate your being.

Three-finger Technique

Bring your thumb and first two fingers of your left hand together to anchor this feeling of deep relaxation. You can use this as a trigger to take you back to this state whenever you need to.

Mindfulness

Observe your thoughts as they stream in and out of your consciousness. Focus your attention on what is going on in the present moment. Be aware of the life force energy circulating through your body. Pay attention to the sounds you hear. Tune in to your heart beating. Then focus on your breathing. Notice the rise and fall of your belly as you breathe deeply and naturally. Observe the breath coming in and going out until that is all that is on your mind. If your mind wanders away from this focus, simply bring it back to your breath.

Body Wisdom

Connect with the wisdom of your body. Ask it what it needs from you to be healthy. Listen for the answer with the intention to act on the message you receive.

Affirmations

End with affirmations, for example:

- My body and mind are strong and healthy and in perfect harmony.
- I commit to caring for my body with plenty of exercise, healthy nutrition, and daily deep relaxation.
- I love and accept my body, unconditionally.

MASTERMINDING

Your thoughts create your reality. Masterminding directs your thoughts towards the reality you desire. You can use this discipline to create your day, year and your life. It is a way of creating what you want rather than what you don't want.

Masterminding is done in a state of deep relaxation. You can practice these mental exercises at the end of Energetics. If you practice Masterminding on its own then you will need to get into a state of relaxation first. Use alternate nostril breathing as described on page 72.

Reflection

Reflection provides the flexibility to change. When you change the way you look at life, your life changes. Look at your life. Decide what you want to create with the energy of your thoughts. Declare it with an "I am" statement, for example, "I am living in my dream home" or "I am enjoying a healthy relationship."

Visualization

Visualization gives you the endurance to keep supporting your actions with helpful thoughts. Get into a state of deep relaxation and imagine what your vision looks like. See as many details as possible. Picture what you look like, what you are doing, and how this affects you and others in your life.

Expanding

Getting to the feeling you associate with having what you want will expand your mind and align your thoughts with your actions. Allow your imagination to take you to the feeling you associate with having this show up in your life. For example, if confidence is the feeling you associate with having a healthy, fit body, then use that mental picture of yourself in that condition to create the feeling of confidence.

Focusing

Focusing on the feeling develops the strength you need to shape your life with the energy vibration of your thoughts. By focusing on your breathing, you will connect what you are feeling with the higher vibrational energy of creativity and intention. As you breathe deeply in and out through your nose, you can reinforce the feeling by silently saying to yourself: " I am . . . confident, happy, peaceful, content, etc., or whatever feeling you associate with your desire.

Alternate Nostril Breathing

This is an excellent technique to get into a state of deep relaxation and focus your mind.

Sitting with your spine straight and eyes closed, rest the index and second finger of your right hand on the center of your forehead between your eyebrows. Close your right nostril with your thumb. Inhale slowly through your left nostril to the count of six. Close your left nostril with your ring finger and hold the breath for four counts, then open your right nostril by removing your thumb and exhale for six counts. Inhale again through the right nostril for six counts. Close your right nostril with you thumb, hold four counts, open the left nostril and exhale six counts.

Inhale through the left nostril for six counts. Continue this rhythmic breathing cycle at a comfortable pace until you feel deeply relaxed.

EMOTIONALIZING

Your emotions are the language of your soul. They let you know if you are on a track of love (high energy vibration) or on a track of fear (low energy vibration). Awareness of this language develops and strengthens the connection with your soul. Releasing negative energy allows you to return to your natural state of love and harmony.

Enhancing what you are feeling provides the endurance to let go of lower energy and move to a higher energy level. Expressing love from your heart gives you the energy to connect with others heart - to - heart.

Awareness

The Five Tibetan Rites will stimulate and tone your energy centers (chakras) to such an extent that you will become more aware of your emotional energy. These exercises also have a detoxing effect on the body. Start slowly with just three repetitions of each exercise for the first week, increasing gradually by adding two each week until you reach 21 repetitions of each exercise.

First Tibetan Rite - Spinning

Stand straight with both arms extended out to the side, palms down, and spin in a clockwise direction. Be sure to focus on one point in front of you before you begin spinning and reconnect with that point as you turn to the right.

Modification - Helicopter: Stand with your feet two-to-three feet apart, slightly turned out, arms up and extended out to the sides. Swing your arms and body loosely and freely from right to left. Turn your body as you pivot on to the ball of your left and then right foot, putting your whole body into the swing. Done at a medium pace.

Resting Position: When you finish spinning, place your palms together with fingers spread, focusing on your thumbs to regain your equilibrium. Go slowly at first, especially if you get dizzy. It does get easier with practice.

Second Tibetan Rite

Lie on your back with palms down. Inhale as you extend your legs straight up, feet flexed. Lift your head off the floor. Exhale as you slowly lower your legs and head back down. Relax a moment and then repeat.

Modification: Bend your knees and extend your legs straight up.

Resting Position: When finished, lie flat on your back in the relaxation pose and rest there for two deep breaths.

Third Tibetan Rite

Kneel with your knees under your hips. Lower your chin down towards your chest while placing your hands just below your buttocks, toes curled under. As you inhale, let your head drop back as far as comfortable, squeeze your shoulder blades together, then return to starting position as you exhale. Repeat.

Modification: Only arch back slightly by looking up and squeezing your shoulder blades together.

Resting Position: With your knees apart (mat width) and feet together, sit on your heels and lower your forehead to the mat with arms outstretched in front of you, and relax there for two deep breaths.

Fourth Tibetan Rite

Sit with legs extended out in front of you, feet flexed. Place your hands flat on the floor by your hips, arms straight, fingers pointing forward. Inhale as you lift your hips into a tabletop position. Don't overarch your back. Let your head fall back and tighten your buttocks. Exhale as you come back to starting position. Repeat.

Modification: Lie on your back with feet close to your buttocks. Raise your hips up and tighten your glutes. Lower back to the floor. Repeat.

Resting Position: Sit with knees bent and soles of your feet together away from your body about 12". Rest your elbows on your inner thighs and release your wrists by rotating them several times in both directions.

Fifth Tibetan Rite

Begin in a push-up position with legs extended and toes curled under, hands under your shoulders and feet shoulder width apart in alignment with your hands. Lower your hips, look up, arch your back, raise your chest, and exhale. Inhale, lift your hips and buttocks up, and lower the head down between your arms making an inverted V. Lower heels toward the floor. Exhale as you return to the first position. Repeat.

Modification: On all fours, look up and arch your back down. Look down and arch your back up. Repeat.

Resting Position: Relax in Child's Pose, knees and feet together, forehead on the mat, arms resting by your sides, hands by your feet.

AWARENESS EXERCISES

Complete these exercises by lying flat on your back in the relaxation pose. Be aware of any physical sensations, i.e., warmth, tingling, tension, or pain. Allow what you are experiencing in your body to guide you to your emotions. Ask "what am I feeling?" Once you identify the feeling, i.e. sadness, ask "what is the message?" The message of sadness could be you need to forgive yourself or someone else.

Releasing

The Spinal Rock will help you release emotional energy that needs to move. Sit with your buttocks close to your feet, hands grasping your legs under your knees. Bring your chin towards your chest and rock back, shoulder blades touching the floor. Let your legs go over your head and back towards the floor. Then rock forward, place your feet on the floor, and exhale deeply. Do seven repetitions.

Enhancing

In a cross-legged seated position with eyes closed, take seven deep breaths to enhance whatever you are feeling. As you breathe in, imagine positive energy coming up from the earth, entering the base of your spine, and going up to the top of your head. As you breathe out, imagine positive energy cleansing your entire body from the top of your head to the base of your spine and back into the earth.

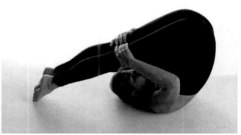

Expression

While in a seated position, inhale as you bring your hands behind your back and clasp them together. Stretch your arms back as you exhale and look up. Hold briefly. Feel your heart center opening.

Place your hands on your knees. Close your eyes and imagine someone you would like to send love to. Send loving energy from your heart to their heart as you breathe deeply.

INNERCISES

Innercises will connect you with your spirit so that you can live your life on purpose.

Acceptance

By accepting your connection to your intuitive, creative energy, you strengthen your spirit. Sit in a comfortable position, either cross-legged on the floor (on a cushion) or in a chair with your spine straight, hands resting on your thighs, palms up. Close your eyes and settle into your physical body, being aware of the support of the earth beneath you. Be aware of your breath. Imagine that your body is completely surrounded by a cocoon of white light. Focus your attention on the crown chakra (spirituality) at the top of your head. As you breathe in, imagine the light streaming in, moving down your spine to your heart center. As you breathe out, imagine the light filling every cell of your body. You can count your breaths by silently saying "breathe in one, breathe out one, breathe in two, breathe out two, etc. Do this until you feel light and relaxed.

Trust

Trust in your intuitive guidance and you will gain the flexibility to make good choices. Focus your attention on your brow chakra (intuition) at the center of your forehead. Silently ask for spiritual guidance. This can be about something specific you are dealing with or about your life in general. Be still and listen. Trust the guidance when you know it is for the highest good of all concerned, including yourself. Trust it enough to follow through with your actions. You can also ask, "How may I serve?"

Gratitude

Gratitude is a daily practice that increases your spiritual endurance. Bring your awareness to the throat chakra (expression). Silently express gratitude for your guidance and anything else you choose to be grateful for in the moment.

Unconditional Love

Unconditional love is the essence of who you really are that sustains the flow of higher vibrational energy coming from your Source. Tune in to your heart chakra (love) in the center of your chest. As you inhale, imagine the light that still surrounds you, streaming in through the top of your head, moving down your spine to your heart center. As you exhale, see that light radiating out into the world. You can use a mantra (instrument of thought), i.e., "I am love" or "breathe in love — breathe out love." When you are finished, be aware of your body and your connection to the earth before you open your eyes.

Grounding Exercise

Stand with your feet shoulder-width apart. As you come up onto your toes, raise your arms up, elbows bent, hands making fists. As you come back down onto your heels, swing your arms down by your sides and say "haaaa." Repeat several times.

STRESS RELIEF PROCESS

Stress can be a catalyst for change. Use this seven-step process to turn resistance into ease.

1) Identify the source of stress:
   Is it something outside of yourself such as another person, traffic, or weather?
   Is it your thoughts?
   Is it something about your body?

2) What am I resisting about this source of stress?

3) Is this something I have the power to change?
   If I can't change it going forward, can I change my response to it?

4) Who would I have to become to make this change?
   What quality do I need to develop?

5) Am I willing to change rather than resist?

6) What's the first step?

7) Do I feel relieved?

Letting go of resistance will bring you back to your natural state of ease. It's worth doing this process as often as needed to prevent chronic stress.

I suggest making a copy of this process to carry with you to use in times of stress. It will be like having me with you as a coach, especially if you can write down your answers.

This is a great way to take your power back. Anything that is causing you to be stressed out has taken your power away.

"No matter what is happening on the outside, the world within holds the key to health and happiness."

- Carol Gutzeit

THE COMMITMENT

To change your life from the inside out takes commitment. As you take the journey to awakening and create a balanced life that you love, you will be making a great contribution not only to yourself, but also to the world. Although it requires self-awareness, self-acceptance, and self-discipline to make a significant change, these things lead to freedom.

Satori Yoga™ is a daily practice that helps you energize your body, mind, heart, and spirit. As you train to strengthen your body, discipline your mind, open your heart, and connect more deeply to your soul for guidance, you will become better equipped to live your life more joyfully.

Life is an incredible journey. Use this book as a guide to tap into your physical, mental, emotional, and spiritual energy resources. When you allow your energy to flow, you will awaken to your full potential. With this awakening comes responsibility. Make the commitment to raise your energy vibration and bring more love into the world. This is the one purpose we can all share that truly makes a difference.

I _____ commit to practicing at least one aspect of Satori Yoga™ each day. I intend to love my body, mind, heart, and spirit and condition myself for endurance, strength, and flexibility. As I awaken the power and wisdom within me, I commit to being a force for good to make a positive difference in the world.

_____   _____
SIGNATURE   DATE

30 DAYS
TO A BALANCED LIFE

Now that you have the tools you need to build a balanced life that you love, here are practical ways to implement what you've learned for the next 30 days. The first week is about loving yourself through self-care. The second week focuses on loving your life and manifesting your dreams. The third week is devoted to loving others by taking responsibility for your emotions. The fourth week is about waking up and remembering who you really are . . . an expression of divine love.

Each day you will have a FOCUS that will direct your mind towards creating a balanced life that you love. A new HEALTHY HABIT will be introduced along with TODAY'S PRACTICE to help you stay on track. A SATORI WISDOM message with an "I Am" mantra will stimulate ideas for taking inspired action. Since thoughts lead to feelings which lead to actions which lead to results, anything you declare after the words "I Am" is very powerful and will set in motion a series of events to shape your reality.

Once you have completed the 30 days, please email me at carol@destinationsatori.com and let me know how you did. I would love to hear from you!

Photographs for Satori Wisdom on the following pages were contributed by:
Nancy Sloane, Nichole Gutzeit, Kathy Smith, Jeremy Sloane, and Carol Gutzeit.

DAY 1

FOCUS

The focus for today is to breathe deeply by expanding your belly as you breathe in and contract it as you breathe out. Really focus on how this feels and how it instantly produces calm, soothing energy in your mind and body.

HEALTHY HABIT

Determine a trigger that will help you remember to take four deep breaths throughout the day. For example, whenever you get up from your desk, while driving in your car, or before you make a phone call, stop and just breathe. As you breathe deeply say to yourself "I am happy to be alive!" Breathe in through your nose four counts, hold four counts, and breathe out through your mouth eight counts. Repeat three more times.

TODAY'S PRACTICE

The breathing exercises that start on page 55 are a great way to feel rejuvenated. You will be exchanging carbon-rich air for fresh oxygen, especially if you can step outdoors for this practice. These exercises are an energizer and instantly clear brain fog.

DAILY RITUAL

Start your day with journaling to get clear and set an intention. End your day with journaling to reflect on your progress.

SATORI WISDOM - I Am Letting Go

I am grateful to past experience for shaping who I am today. I thank those who have been part of my world. Their actions, choices, and behaviors have been great teachers. Looking back I see my pain disappear into dust behind me and welcome wisdom in its place. Letting go of attachment to specific outcomes, frees me to take the high road and enjoy the larger view.

DAY 2

FOCUS
Notice where in your body you are holding on to tension and breathe into it. As you breathe out, let that tension go. Being relaxed in your body and mind creates a state of ease that flows into your whole life.

HEALTHY HABIT
Accept what is happening in each moment and smile frequently for a natural release of endorphins.

TODAY'S PRACTICE
Continue practicing the breathing exercises and add on the yoga sequence that starts on page 58. "Salutation to the Moon" has two variations dedicated to the full moon and new moon.

DAILY RITUAL
Practice "Salutation to the Moon" outdoors under the moon (weather permitting) or create a sacred space in your home for practicing yoga and include your favorite music.

SATORI WISDOM - I Am Flexible
I have an agile body, mind, heart, and spirit, and can adapt to life's unexpected twists and turns. I remain focused on what I want without attaching to end results. Each experience helps me stretch, strengthen, and increase my flexibility. Knowing I can handle whatever comes along, I am ready to take a leap of faith.

DAY 3

FOCUS

It is extremely beneficial to receive bodywork from a skilled professional on a regular basis. Massage will enhance your circulation, release toxins, promote relaxation, and instill a sense of well-being. Take care of your body to keep it running smoothly and enhance everything you do.

HEALTHY HABIT

Schedule a professional massage or ask for a foot rub.

TODAY'S PRACTICE

Do the self-massage that starts on page 67 and incorporate hand reflexology into your day for an energy boost.

DAILY RITUAL

Use an essential oil, i.e., lavender, lemon, or peppermint, to enhance the self-massage or foot rub.

SATORI WISDOM - I Am Energetic

My life force energy compels me to move forward and continually search for what sustains me. Life energizes me to live in harmony with the forces of nature. As a spirited energetic being, I am attracting what I seek.

DAY 4

FOCUS

There is an ancient Chinese proverb that says: "Relaxation is who you really are. Tension is who you think you should be." These are words to live by. There is always going to be more to do. When we live our lives just trying to get everything done, we miss the enjoyment of living. You will be much more effective in everything you do if you can relax and be present.

HEALTHY HABIT

Make a TO DO and a TO BE list. Assign numbers to each item on your list in order of their priority. Decide what qualities and feelings you need in order to be at ease as you complete your tasks.

TODAY'S PRACTICE

Today take ten to fifteen minutes for deep relaxation using the techniques described on page 70.

DAILY RITUAL

Create a tranquil space for relaxation in your home, office, or outdoors. This could be a hammock, a comfortable recliner, a yoga mat, or cushions on the floor in a quiet environment. Make this your peaceful sanctuary where you retreat to daily.

SATORI WISDOM - I Am Relaxed

Today is a day for re-charging, resting, and being still. I find a quiet spot to relax and do not feel compelled to do anything. Rest is as important to a balanced, healthy life as doing. I take time to unwind and just chill.

DAY 5

FOCUS

You are what you eat! When you choose whole foods, you are adding to the wholeness of your body. There is such a variety of colorful fruits and veggies that all have healing properties. A plant-based, whole foods diet is the foundation of a natural way to nourish your body and provide it with the fuel it needs to be healthy.

HEALTHY HABIT

When you eat whole foods, notice how good you feel and be grateful for the abundance of natural foods that are available to you. Take time to slow down and eat consciously, and you will derive even more benefits from your food. Drink a large glass of water with two teaspoons of organic apple cider vinegar with the "mother" in it 15 minutes before each meal to aid in digestion. Add one teaspoon of stevia or honey to sweeten.

TODAY'S PRACTICE

Practice deep breathing before each meal and experience the mind/body connection that supports your natural state of well-being. This will relax your nervous system and aid in digestion. Breathe in four counts through your nose and out eight counts through your mouth. Do four repetitions.

DAILY RITUAL

Bless your food and give thanks for the nourishment it provides.

SATORI WISDOM - I Am Natural

It is perfectly natural for my body to feel relaxed and flexible, and my mind to be creative and spontaneous. It feels good when my heart is open to both giving and receiving love, allowing my spirit to be free to enjoy life. I am living in harmony when I remember my true nature.

DAY 6

FOCUS
We are living in a physical world and it's important to stay connected to the earth. When we are too caught up in our thinking and living in our heads, we miss out on the present moment, where life is happening.

HEALTHY HABIT
Make a conscious connection to the earth. Stand barefoot on the ground and feel the support of the earth beneath you. Breathe in the energy through the soles of your feet and breathe out anything you need to release.

TODAY'S PRACTICE
Practice the breathing exercises on page 55 outdoors.

DAILY RITUAL
Do a walking meditation in nature and synchronize your breathing to the rhythm of your movement.

SATORI WISDOM - I Am Grounded
I feel the richness of the earth beneath my feet and relish the strength that comes from being rooted in place. Stability does not come from somewhere out there. I stand solidly in the landscape of my life as it appears in the light of today.

DAY 7

FOCUS

Congratulations on completing the first week of your journey to a balanced life! This time has been devoted to taking care of yourself with ways to reduce stress, release tension, eat healthy, and increase endurance. Today is about acknowledging all that you have done to create balance and feel rejuvenated. Well done!

HEALTHY HABIT

Reward yourself in a healthy and satisfying way.

TODAY'S PRACTICE

When you practice Energetics, be aware of the life force energy that is moving through your body and keeping you alive!

DAILY RITUAL

Write in your journal about how far you've come this week.

SATORI WISDOM - I Am Balanced

I acknowledge my body's perfection with gratitude for being such a good host to my mind, heart, and spirit. I release any negative thoughts I may have about myself or others, and thank the Universe for my beauty and strength. I honor the way everything in me harmonizes with the outside world, and stand perfectly balanced from an expanded perspective.

DAY 8

FOCUS

Take time for reflection. When you look at your life, see what is being reflected back to you in the way of relationships, career, health, and abundance. Get clear about what you want in all areas of your life and then set your intention with an "I am" statement.

HEALTHY HABIT

Brainstorming, as described on page 38 is a great way to engage your right brain and allow thoughts and ideas to flow. Follow that with a written description using the left side of your brain. Get in the habit of using both sides of your brain to develop mental wholeness.

TODAY'S PRACTICE

Practice saying your "I Am" mantra and read your written description.

DAILY RITUAL

Journal about your dreams and desires, and how you feel about manifesting them.

SATORI WISDOM - I Am Clear

Sometimes I don't see things as they truly are. The ego has a funny way of blurring reality to protect itself. Whenever the signal is out of focus, I employ patience and let the clarity come. I always know what is right for me. Sometimes I just need to let the noise die down to see it.

DAY 9

FOCUS
Everything is created twice, first in the mind and then in the physical world. Your imagination is your best creative resource. Use it wisely and it will help you manifest anything your heart desires. Visualize what you have declared for your life and remember, what you imagine you can also create!

HEALTHY HABIT
When you first wake up in the morning, spend a few minutes visualizing how you would like your day to go.

TODAY'S PRACTICE
Use Alternate Nostril Breathing on page 72 to calm your nervous system and get into a relaxed state of mind. Then practice visualization.

DAILY RITUAL
Use The Four Questions as you fall asleep tonight: What am I proud of? What am I grateful for? What am I looking forward to? What am I committed to?

SATORI WISDOM - I Am Imaginative
What I imagine I can also create. I use my imagination to move into the reality I desire. I focus on what I choose to manifest and move confidently in the direction of my dreams. My imagination takes me wherever I want to go.

DAY 10

FOCUS
Everything you want in life has a feeling associated with it. When you get to the feeling first and BE the feeling, then you will DO what that feeling inspires you to do and allow yourself to HAVE what you associate with that feeling. Focus on feeling good!

HEALTHY HABIT
Be aware of your mood. A good mood is the best time to take action. A bad mood means it's time to change your thinking. Look for what's going right in your life instead of what's going wrong.

TODAY'S PRACTICE
Practice the breathing exercises on page 55 to feel energized.

DAILY RITUAL
Make a vision board that inspires you. Look at it daily and feel good about your vision.

SATORI WISDOM - I Am Feeling
My emotions are guideposts to what is right for me. I open a window and welcome them in! Even those that may not feel good will serve me. Whenever I feel an uncomfortable feeling, I just nod and wink and observe the information my body is giving me. It knows what I need. I trust my heart to lead me where I need to go.

DAY 11

FOCUS

Masterminding is a four-step creative process. First you must get clear and declare what you want. Then you visualize and imagine having it. Next, get to the feeling of what it's like to have it. The final step is to feel good in the present moment and allow what you want to manifest. These mental exercises train your mind to focus on thoughts that create good feelings in the present while you move in the direction of your vision. Use this mental discipline to create what you desire.

HEALTHY HABIT

Come to your senses! Your power is in the present moment. Engage your five senses throughout the day to connect your mind with your body to become present.

TODAY'S PRACTICE

Practice Masterminding (Reflect, Visualize, Expand, Focus) and focus throughout the day on the feeling of having what you desire.

DAILY RITUAL

Smile when you look in the mirror tonight and say, "All is well." Recall everything that went well today.

SATORI WISDOM - I Am Focused

Instinctively I know what to do and do it. When I attend to the task at hand, everything fits together perfectly. As part of a larger community, I see the value of my essential nature. I am focused on collaborating with others and doing my part to build a better world.

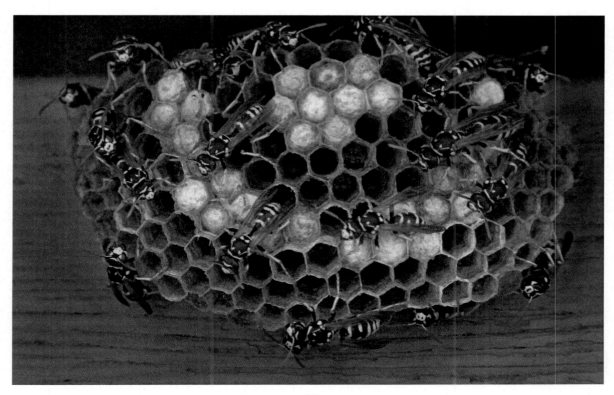

DAY 12

FOCUS

Just as physical exercise shapes your body, mental exercise shapes your life. Put the two together and you will get the best results. Use visualization when you practice strength training to maximize your workout, and imagine what your body looks and feels like being strong, lean, healthy, and fit.

HEALTHY HABIT

Incorporate strength training into your day and get into the habit of exercising two to three times per week. You can use your own body weight, free weights, machines, bands, water resistance exercises, or Kettlebells.

TODAY'S PRACTICE

Use the self-massage on page 67 to send energy to your muscles before strength training.

DAILY RITUAL

Stretch after your workout and pay attention to how your body feels as you become stronger and more flexible.

SATORI WISDOM - I Am Strong

I am confident in my ability to be self-reliant. Looking back, I see how I've come through for myself time and again. No matter what comes up, I will rise to the occasion. Strength comes from within.

DAY 13

FOCUS

When you feed your brain the nutrients it needs to thrive, you tend to think more clearly and make better choices. Better choices lead to a lifestyle that supports who you really are and reflects your brilliance. Get your omega-3s today and your brain will thank you.

HEALTHY HABIT

Choose good sources of protein that nourish your brain, i.e., nuts (especially walnuts), seeds (flaxseed, chia, pumpkin), beans, tofu, tempeh, eggs, and wild salmon.

TODAY'S PRACTICE

Practice taking three deep cleansing breaths before eating. Breathe in through your nose four counts, hold four, exhale eight counts.

DAILY RITUAL

Consume virgin coconut oil (1 to 3 tablespoons) daily for amazing health benefits. Cook with it and add it to your food, smoothies, and hot beverages. You can also use it topically.

SATORI WISDOM - I Am Brilliant

Sometimes we are Evergreens, growing slowly, steadily, appearing mostly the same year after year. Sometimes we are the Aspen, rapidly spinning off tendrils, shedding leaves or growing new ones, changing colors season to season. Both are brilliant ways of being. Dazzling appearances can be deceiving. Whatever stage of development you are in, gently allow your brilliance to shine. Green is a beautiful color too.

DAY 14

FOCUS
Rather than monitoring your thoughts all day, just notice how you feel. Your thoughts create your feelings and when you're not feeling good, that's a cue to check your thinking. If you're focused on something you don't like that isn't going right in your life, use this awareness as an opportunity to reframe what's happening and tell yourself a different story that feels better.

HEALTHY HABIT
Check in with how you're feeling throughout the day and notice the thoughts that are creating those feelings.

TODAY'S PRACTICE
Use The Four Questions as needed on page 36 to shift your focus and feel better.

DAILY RITUAL
Use an empty frame to look at your surroundings from different perspectives.

SATORI WISDOM - I Am Reframing
Today I choose to reframe those experiences that appear to be causing my unhappiness or discontent. I can either see through the prison of my fearful thoughts or with the clarity of my higher self. Reframing to a higher perspective allows me to see that this is a friendly universe. I can change my perspective any time I choose.

DAY 15

FOCUS

Awareness is the first step towards change. You really can't make any changes until you are aware of the need to do so. Being aware of your emotions and what they mean is like learning a foreign language - the language of your soul. Once you see how useful it is to look at your emotions from this higher perspective, it will become easier to learn this amazing language.

HEALTHY HABIT

Place your hand on the center of your chest, take three deep breaths, and ask, "What am I feeling?"

TODAY'S PRACTICE

Practice Emotionalizing described on page 72. Start with three repetitions the first week. Add two per week until you reach 21 repetitions.

DAILY RITUAL

Journal about your emotions and their messages. Notice when you are operating from a track of love or fear. Set your course for love and welcome any guidance you receive about being on or off course.

SATORI WISDOM - I Am Aware

Sometimes we think we need to be something other than who we already are and don't notice the magnificence of who we are right now. I am aware of my unique beauty and celebrate my true colors. The more I connect with my core essence, the more beautiful I become.

DAY 16

FOCUS
Pay attention to the signals you get throughout the day, whether they take the form of emotions or physical symptoms. Once you get the message, you can let go of the unpleasant emotion or physical sensation. This is how you get to the cause rather than just dealing with symptoms.

HEALTHY HABIT
Use deep sighing throughout the day as a way to release stuck emotions.

TODAY'S PRACTICE
Practice the spinal rock on page 75 as a way to release stored emotional tension.

DAILY RITUAL
Continue to journal about your emotions by writing "I am feeling . . ." and then just allow what comes through to be released on paper.

SATORI WISDOM - I Am Releasing
I am seeking higher ground and releasing my fear of the unknown. There is always a solid place to land wherever I go. Change is easy when I loosen my grip on old beliefs and allow new thoughts to emerge. I feel strong and safe as I release tension, and create a new perspective.

DAY 17

FOCUS

Enthusiasm comes from the Greek word "entheos" which means to be filled with God. Just saying "I Am Enthusiastic" connects you with this high vibration. Use this mantra throughout the day along with deep breathing and good posture, and you will be aligned with your authentic self.

HEALTHY HABIT

Use your vocabulary to elevate your mood. When someone asks, "How are you today?" and you're feeling good, take it up a notch and say "I'm great!"

TODAY'S PRACTICE

Use the Emotional Energy Process (EEP) on page 48 to track your emotions back to your beliefs. You may want to write the process on a 3x5 card and carry it with you.

DAILY RITUAL

Be aware of negative emotion and journal yourself through it using the Emotional Energy Process. Be aware of how it feels to change a limiting belief.

SATORI WISDOM - I Am Enthusiastic

I am passionate about life and give love to everything I do. My body, mind, and heart soar with the joy of my spirit when I do what I love and love what I do. I elevate others when I live by example. Enthusiasm is contagious.

DAY 18

FOCUS
One of the limiting beliefs that can hold us back from giving and receiving love is that we are unlovable. Your negative emotions will alert you to your negative thoughts and beliefs. Emotions are your guidance system so pay attention to all of them.

HEALTHY HABIT
Remember that you are lovable and express your love to others today so they can remember how lovable they are.

TODAY'S PRACTICE
Practice the fourth part of Emotionalizing on page 75 or all of it beginning on page 72. Open your heart and send love to someone you care about.

DAILY RITUAL
Write 10 things you love about yourself. Now write 10 things you love about another person, particularly someone who has been a challenge for you to love.

SATORI WISDOM - I Am Lovable
I was born lovable. If I ever doubt the truth of this, it is because of a story I have told myself. Past experience does not determine who I am. I am ready to feel valued and loved. I attract love simply by being me.

DAY 19

FOCUS

There is nothing quite like eating healthy food that is made with love. When you go to the grocery store and purchase all the colorful produce that is available, think about all the love that went into growing those fruits and veggies.

HEALTHY HABIT

Eat an abundance of plant-based whole foods and include some raw vegan food at every meal.

TODAY'S PRACTICE

Practice Emotionalizing on page 72 to stimulate and tone your chakras, and reverse aging.

DAILY RITUAL

As you prepare your meals today, put loving energy into your food. Take a moment to bless it and be grateful for its nourishment.

SATORI WISDOM - I Am Nourished

The universe is a source of abundant nourishment. I choose to eat more greens and foods rich in color to keep my body strong and healthy. I remember to also nourish my soul with uplifting thoughts and experiences.

DAY 20

FOCUS
The ability to move and think quickly comes easily and naturally when you have a yoga practice. Yoga means yoke or union. It's a way of connecting the mind with the body in the present moment. Staying agile in each moment after you leave your mat will create a feeling of confidence in everything you do.

HEALTHY HABIT
Get up from sitting at least once every 30 minutes to stretch.

TODAY'S PRACTICE
Practice yoga with a DVD or attend a class.

DAILY RITUAL
When you step onto a yoga mat, set an intention for your practice.

SATORI WISDOM - I Am Agile
I am agile of body and mind, flexing and stretching beyond my boundaries. I follow a daily practice that allows for change and welcomes challenges. Agility keeps me young and vibrant!

DAY 21

FOCUS
Whatever you want more of in your life, give more of that to others. If you want more joy then share your joy with the world. There is joy within you. It is your natural state and one of the highest vibrational frequencies on the emotional scale.

HEALTHY HABIT
Smile at everyone you encounter today and that includes when you look in the mirror.

TODAY'S PRACTICE
Connect with your joy as you practice Emotionalizing and feel your heart opening up to let more joy in.

DAILY RITUAL
End your day with an uplifting story, even if you have to write it.

SATORI WISDOM - I Am Joy
I live life with an open heart and offer a vibration of pure joy. Whatever direction I choose to go and for however long I decide to stay, I bring joy to others. I drink in the sweetness of life with every breath and every connection I make.

DAY 22

FOCUS
Spending time in silence is a way to stay open to receiving guidance from your higher self and tap into the abundance of the Universe. When you accept that you are a spiritual being having a human experience, there is a shift in consciousness that frees your spirit and allows you to encounter the miraculous.

HEALTHY HABIT
Let go of judgment and accept others just as they are by looking for the positive intention behind their behavior.

TODAY'S PRACTICE
Practice Innercises on page 76 as a way to experience acceptance.

DAILY RITUAL
Journal about acceptance and how good it feels.

SATORI WISDOM - I Am Silent
My powers of observation are heightened in silent contemplation. I see the truth clearly and intuit what is right for me in any situation. I know how to find the light when surrounded by darkness.

DAY 23

FOCUS

When you quiet your mind and go into the stillness, simply ask for guidance and you will receive it. Guidance comes in a variety of ways, and one of them is through your intuition. This is a gut feeling or a knowing that goes beyond logic or reason. Your intuitive voice gets stronger the more you pay attention to it. The more you listen and trust your guidance enough to follow it, the higher your self-esteem will be.

HEALTHY HABIT

Trust your intuition enough to act on it.

TODAY'S PRACTICE

Practice Innercises on page 76 and ask for guidance.

DAILY RITUAL

Journal about the guidance you received today.

SATORI WISDOM - I Am Intuitive

I trust my instincts. My intuition connects me to the highest good for myself and others. No one can tell me what is best for me or show me my path. I pay close attention to how my body feels when I contemplate a decision, and let the answers come. Any action I take when I rely on my intuition for guidance, is perfect. I jot down my intention, take my time, and allow my intuitive self to drive.

DAY 24

FOCUS
Being in a state of gratitude throughout the day keeps you feeling happy because you are focused on what you DO have rather than what you DON'T. There is so much to be grateful for that it's an easy practice to add to your life. Remember, where your attention goes, energy flows.

HEALTHY HABIT
Express appreciation to someone with a phone call, card, or gift.

TODAY'S PRACTICE
Practice Innercises on page 76 and focus on feeling grateful.

DAILY RITUAL
Write five things you are grateful for today.

SATORI WISDOM - I Am Gratitude
My heart is filled with the blessings of the world. Everywhere I look, there is beauty, wonder, and delight to thrill my senses. All is given to me and fills me with gratitude.

DAY 25

FOCUS
When you give love to yourself and others unconditionally it feels good! Love is the essence of who you really are, and when you express love without conditions or expectations, it connects you with your natural way of being. Share this authentic love with the world and watch the miracles unfold!

HEALTHY HABIT
Let go of the need to control others and love them unconditionally.

TODAY'S PRACTICE
Practice Innercises and allow love to flow through you.

DAILY RITUAL
Journal about what it means to love unconditionally.

SATORI WISDOM - I Am Love
Love is my eternal essence. It is the energy that creates, connects, heals, and expands my being. I give and receive love freely to allow this divine energy to flow and flourish. Loving thoughts are at the heart of feeling good, which lets me know when I'm aligned with my higher self.

DAY 26

FOCUS

Life is a great adventure! Get out there today and do something you've never done before. Love whatever you choose to do, and you will experience a healing energy throughout your entire being. One of my favorite sayings is: "Fear knocked on the door, love answered, and no one was there." When you love your life you become unstoppable!

HEALTHY HABIT

Try something new! Go somewhere you've never been, meet new people, learn a new skill, hobby, or sport.

TODAY'S PRACTICE

Practice Innercises and ask for guidance on the best adventure for you today.

DAILY RITUAL

Journal about your adventure and what it feels like to be unstoppable.

SATORI WISDOM - I Am Unstoppable

Life is a series of peaks and valleys. When I reach one of its peaks, I feel unstoppable. Going through the valleys makes this peak experience more enjoyable. I gain strength from the climb and discover a new perspective at the top. By seeing how far I've come, I'm inspired to use challenges to continue the climb. Nothing can stop me now!

DAY 27

FOCUS
Devote one day this week (perhaps today) to cleanse your body and mind with lemon water, fresh juices, smoothies, and vegan soups. This allows your digestive system a chance to rest, and gives you mental clarity and peace of mind.

HEALTHY HABIT
Drink hot lemon water first thing in the morning to create a healthy alkaline state in your body. You can sweeten it with organic grade B maple syrup or organic raw honey.

TODAY'S PRACTICE
Practice Innercises as a way to start your day off feeling connected to your spirit.

DAILY RITUAL
Journal about what you need to let go of in your life, i.e., clutter, things you no longer use, toxic relationships, toxic beliefs, or bad habits.

SATORI WISDOM - I Am Cleansed
Change is inevitable. I can either accept the washing away of the old, or struggle as it occurs. When I surrender to the current and go with the flow without resisting its natural course, I am cleansed of suffering. The force of life is out of my control, and I accept whatever comes my way.

DAY 28

FOCUS
Whenever you get caught up in the fast pace of the human race and feel pressured to do more or have more, remember to stop and observe what is going on in your inner world on a physical, mental, and emotional level. Connect with the part of you that is observing your body, mind, and emotions . . . your spirit.

HEALTHY HABIT
Live from the inside out. Remember that the outer world is a reflection of your inner world.

TODAY'S PRACTICE
Practice Innercises and observe your inner world.

DAILY RITUAL
Write from the observer point of view and your spiritual perspective.

SATORI WISDOM - I Am the Observer
When I take a step back from what is happening and observe my thoughts and behavior, I can see patterns from past conditioning that no longer serve me. When I activate my inner observer, I disengage from the drama, and my ego instantly loses its power over me. This realization expands my consciousness and allows me to make immediate changes to my behavior while revealing that I am more than the one being observed. I am also the observer.

DAY 29

FOCUS
The journey to awakening is about expansion. Fear contracts your energy and love expands it. You get to choose the way you want to go through life, moment by moment.

HEALTHY HABIT
In any situation or encounter ask yourself "what would love say or do?"

TODAY'S PRACTICE
Practice the part of Satori Yoga™ that makes you feel expansive. If possible, practice outdoors.

DAILY RITUAL
Give and receive at least six hugs today.

SATORI WISDOM - I Am Expansive
There is a place within me where the earth meets the sky, reminding me that I am both physical and non-physical. My physical self is solid like a rock. My non-physical self is expansive and unlimited. This duality enables me to grow and evolve.

DAY 30

FOCUS
Although this 30-day journey has come to an end, your life journey continues. As you move forward feel the sense of wholeness you have created by removing blocks and becoming more connected with your body, mind, heart, and spirit. You have always been whole and now you know it!

HEALTHY HABIT
Only use positive words after "I am" so that you are empowering yourself when you speak.

TODAY'S PRACTICE
Practice all of Satori Yoga™ to experience wholeness.

DAILY RITUAL
Journal about your journey to a balanced life and how far you've come in 30 days.

SATORI WISDOM - I Am Whole
I experience wholeness when I allow the masculine and feminine aspects to come into balance and alignment. My feminine, receptive side attracts information that becomes the source of wisdom for my masculine, active side to powerfully manifest what I desire. When this happens, I feel on top of the world!

CONGRATULATIONS!

Dear Reader,

Congratulations on completing your 30-day journey to a balanced life! This has been a gradual, day-by-day commitment to living with more ease and grace. You can use this 30-day program over and over again, or you can choose from the following options to help you continue creating a balanced life that you love:

- Add the Satori Yoga™ DVD to help with your daily practice.
- Sign up for the next "30 Days to a Balanced Life" online group coaching program.
- Subscribe to the Destination Satori YouTube channel for free 2-minute yoga videos at https://www.youtube.com/user/destinationsatori/videos.
- Go to: www.destinationsatori.com/assessment to take the online assessment and receive a free introductory coaching session.
- Attend a Satori Living Retreat.
- Become certified as a Satori Lifestyle Coach.
- Become certified as a Satori Yoga™ teacher.

It is my deepest wish that this book will help you transform your life. Experience is the greatest teacher, and that is why I've included this 30-day program as a guide to creating your best life.

With love and gratitude,

Carol Gutzeit

ABOUT THE AUTHOR

Carol is the founder of Destination Satori LLC, a lifestyle coaching company in Evergreen, Colorado, and the originator of Satori Lifestyle Coaching™ and Satori Yoga™ offering certifications in both professions. Her unique program has been transforming people's lives since 1989 when she started Satori Hawaii, Inc., a corporate wellness company. As a corporate trainer and motivational speaker, Carol has addressed large audiences for such companies as Pitney Bowes, Home Depot, Ampol, Data General, Verifone, McDonald's, and United Parcel Service. She has also presented seminars and training programs to groups at public and private schools, universities, government agencies, resorts, spas, and health clubs. Her stress reduction program, Energetics, has been featured on Hawaiian Airlines as part of the in-flight entertainment. As a personal trainer and lifestyle coach, she has worked with individuals ranging from the physically challenged to dedicated athletes who have experienced life-changing results. Carol started out on a personal quest for physical fitness that evolved into a passion for creating a balanced life. She teaches individuals and groups how to reconnect with their personal power and inner wisdom so they can create a lifestyle that supports their health, happiness, and peace of mind. Carol created "30 Days to a Balanced Life" as an online coaching program to reach people across the country and around the world in the comfort and convenience of their homes. For more information on Destination Satori's coaching, certification and licensing programs, retreats, workshops, classes, and products, go to destinationsatori.com.